THE PASSING OF EMPIRE

First published 1913
This edition published by Lector House in 2023

ISBN: 978-93-5800-766-4

Lector House LLP
Registered Office: H. No. 96, Block C, Tomar Colony,
Burari, Delhi – 110084, India
info@lectorhouse.com
www.lectorhouse.com

THE PASSING OF EMPIRE

HAROLD FIELDING-HALL

2023

LECTOR HOUSE LLP

THE PASSING OF EMPIRE

BY

H. FIELDING-HALL

AUTHOR OF "THE SOUL OF A PEOPLE"
"THE HEARTS OF MEN," ETC.

"Man shall not live by bread alone, but by every word
that proceedeth out of the mouth of God"—
that is to say by ideas

PREFACE

Most people when they talk of India, most books when they treat of India, are concerned with its differences from the rest of the world. It is the appearance and the dress of its peoples, their customs and habits, their superstitions and religions, that are explained and wondered at.

That is not so here. In this book little or nothing is said of any of these matters; they do not interest me; they are superficial, and I do not care for surface things; they are what divide, and truth is what unites.

It is of the humanity which India shares with the rest of the world, the hearts that beat always the same under whatever skin, the ideals that can never be choked by no matter what customs or religions, that this book is concerned with.

India sees life through different windows than we do; but her eyes are as our eyes, and she has the same desires as we have. She has been nearly dead or sleeping for long, but at last she moves. She is awake or waking. Should it not be our task, our pleasure and our pride, to help her early steps along the path of conscious strength that leads to a national life such as that we have been proud of? And to do so must we not try to understand her?

Have we ever tried?

I do not think we have; but the time is coming when, unless we can go hand in hand with her along her path to nationhood, she will desert us. Her destiny is calling her; shall we keep her back?

We cannot keep her back. "No one can be more wise than Destiny." And if we stand in her way, who will suffer like we shall? For her sake and for ours should we not try to understand?

This book is an attempt at a beginning.

CONTENTS

PART I
THE OLD INDIA

CHAPTER I

INDIAN UNREST

We do not hear so much of the discontent in India now as we did three or four years ago. There are no reports of seditious meetings, incendiary propaganda, or disloyal tendencies. The attempt upon the Viceroy is declared to be an isolated act, springing from no general cause; a sporadic outbreak of crime which has no importance. No special measures have to be taken, nor special legislation passed, though the old repressive legislation is not repealed. In the English daily papers there is little said of India, and no news is said to be good news. Therefore in public estimation India has fallen back from her temporary fever into the immemorial apathy of the East. She is content, and no one need trouble himself about her. The sedition was but a froth upon the surface, it had no deep-lying causes; it was temporary, local, unimportant. We need trouble ourselves no more about it.

There could be no greater nor more fatal mistake.

There may have been outbursts of irritation like that over the Bengal partition which have passed because the cause was removed; we may be now in the trough and not upon the crest of a wave, but that is all that can be said. The discontent has not passed, nor will it, nor can it pass. It is deep-rooted in the very nature of things as they are now. It is not local, nor is it confined to one or two strata of society, nor is it directed against one or two acts of Government. It is universal, in all provinces, in all classes, directed not against this act or that act, but against the Government as a whole. This is very evident to those upon the spot, has been evident for many years. The reason more has not been said about it is the absurd notion that talking of the discontent will tend to increase it, as if real discontent ever arose from words, or as if it could be understood unless it were talked about. It should also be evident to those not upon the spot who reflect on causes and effects. For instance, could the partition of Bengal have raised such a sudden flame had there been peace before? People in neither the East nor the West are roused into such sudden and fierce anger by an administrative change even if the change is not to their tastes. For there was no real change of government, nor substantive hardship. The hardship was sentimental hardship at the worst, not the less a real hardship for that.

No. There was discontent before, and the partition only fanned it into flame.

And that discontent is not sudden. It has grown slowly for many years. It is not local; in one province it may be more apparent than in another, but it is universal. It is not temporary, but increases. So much is admitted by those who know. Yet no one thinks of diagnosing it. They shut their eyes, they sit upon the safety-valve, they give measures which they hope will cause relief but which cannot do so; they merely accentuate the difficulty and emphasise the ignorance that is behind it on both sides. How can you cure a fever unless you diagnose the cause or causes? To administer a drug at random is not likely to succeed, yet what are the Councils but a random drug? How can they act? No one knows what the patient suffers from; she herself least of all, I think. No one can truly diagnose his own illness nor prescribe his remedy. India feels uncomfortable, and clamours for anything she can get. The Indian Government gives her what it can, offering profusest condolence, which is sincere; and for the rest sitting upon her chest.

But that will avail nothing—how can it? The fever is deep-seated, it is remittent, it affects the whole system. It is becoming dangerous both to the patient and her physician. For their lots are bound together. India cannot yet do without us. She has not got the organism to govern herself yet. She has no structure, but is an inchoate mass of people. Did we part, India could not protect herself against her neighbours by sea or land. She would be a prey to any enterprising Power. Internally she would dissolve into anarchy. No one, I think, doubts this. Some claim to doubt it—do they?

And as to England, what would we be were India reft from us?

Further, there is this: you cannot hold India by force alone. Force has its place, but it cannot stand alone. We conquered and have governed India by the consent of the people. In fact, she conquered herself and gave herself to us. We never had to fight peoples, except in Upper Burma, but only Governments—effete, discredited and weak. The peoples accepted us: if not with gladness, yet they did accept. Without that acquiescence we could have done nothing. This must be thoroughly realised, for it is an essential truth. Anyone can see it for himself. Given any superiority you like to assume of Englishman over Indian, could a handful of English officials and seventy thousand or less British troops conquer and rule three hundred-and-fifty millions of people, living in a climate suitable to them but deadly to us, against their will? It is impossible, incredible, absurd. There has been always a tacit and generally an active consent. Now that consent is disappearing. Why? And what is to be done? It must be discovered.

Therefore what I propose to do in this book is: First, to show what our rule was at first and why it was so successful.

> To explain how these factors of success gradually disappeared, while at the same time the people progressed.
>
> To show briefly the state of things to-day—how widely Government and the people have drifted apart, and how unsuitable Government has become.
>
> To examine the cures proposed and indicate how useless they must be.

Finally, to show how alone Government and the people can be brought into harmony and the legitimate desires of both be fulfilled.

Let us go back on history, and recount the past so that we may explain the present.

Some hundreds of years ago—it varies for different places—there were in India kingdoms that were stable and strong and free. The peoples were enterprising, active and intelligent, and a high degree of civilisation was common throughout all classes. I don't think it is generally realised that five or six hundred years ago India was ahead of Europe in most matters.

Gradually all this decayed. How and why it decayed this is not the place to explain; there were several causes, the principal being religion; but these systems of government all crumbled into dust. It was not merely dynasties or ruling classes that passed, but that the whole fabric of its civilisation became weakened and lifeless. The organisms that held the people together dissolved, and instead of kingdoms India became simply a mass of village communities, with no organism above that.

Into this more or less anarchical country came the Moguls from the north, and established an empire. This Empire was accepted for the same reason that ours subsequently was accepted—because the people wanted first of all peace; and as peace could only be found under a strong government, and the Mogul was the only strong power, they accepted it. They had, moreover, no organisations to enable them to resist.

But this Mogul power had no root in the soil, not in any soil. It had cut itself away from its base, and it could not become rooted in India. It had, therefore, never any real vitality. The Normans in England coalesced with the people after a time, and drew strength from them and their institutions, but the Mogul Empire did not.

Nevertheless, it did to a certain extent enlist the people on its side, accept them into its organism. There was in the early Emperors no fanaticism. "As tolerant as Akbar" almost became a proverb. Hindus and Mussulmans worked together in harmony for the benefit of the Empire. That is why it succeeded at all, because the line of division was almost ignored. Then came the fanatic Aurungzebe, who by his zeal for religion began the destruction of the Empire, which came very quickly. And when the ruling power was weakened and began to pass, nothing remained. It was simply a government from above. It had built up no system; it was the head of no organism. When its rulers weakened there was nothing to support them. A king in England might be weak or be deposed, but the nation's life went on because the organism was not dependent entirely on the head. Its strength came from below, not above.

Very rapidly the government was dissolved in all but name, became effete, corrupt, and useless.

Then came the East India Company and overthrew it, establishing a new domination. This again was actively or passively accepted by the people because they wanted peace and order, which are the first wants of all humanity.

This English government was still more foreign than the Mogul domination, but it had one great advantage, it was rooted in the soil. Not in the soil of India, of course, but in that of England. It was a branch of the English tree of government which had its roots deep down in English life. Therefore it had and has a strong vitality. It established over India such peace and order as had never been known.

To do this it had to establish a complete system of government, for there was none of the old machinery left.

It did this on the English fashion. I do not mean that it borrowed the English system. At the beginning it did try this, as the Municipality of Madras and the Permanent Settlement of Bengal show. But so obviously was this absurd that it discontinued transplanting, and framed a system of its own. This was, of course, adapted to the circumstances. Like the Mogul system it was a government from above. It hung, as it were, suspended from the Viceroy and Council. It had no roots in the soil in India; it was not and is not indigenous in any way. Its vitality is derived from England, transmitted through the Secretary of State and the Viceroy. That is the way its life-blood circulates. Were that artery cut, the whole system would die at once. The connection severed, in a few months there would not be a vestige left of the whole great fabric of the Indian Government.

If you follow the current of responsibility you will see that this is so. The lowest official in the Indian hierarchy is the Township officer. He is in charge of, say, two or three hundred square miles of country. To whom is he responsible—the people under him? Not in the least. He is responsible to the Subdivisional officer, he to the District officer, and he—either directly or through the Commissioner—to the Local Government. The Local Governments are responsible to the Viceroy in Council, he to the Secretary of State in England, the Secretary to the Prime Minister, he to Parliament, and Parliament to the constituencies. Where do the Indian people come in? Nowhere.

Again, take responsibility of another kind. Suppose India is attacked—who is responsible for its safety—India? Not so. It is the English people, who defend it with ships, with troops, with money. India, for instance, has no credit in herself. The Indian Government gets credit as a branch of the English Government, with English credit behind it. If the Indian peoples pay it is because England makes them pay, not because by the system of government there is any responsibility to pay.

The government of India has no existence apart from England. It is only 'Indian' inasmuch as it governs India, not that it proceeds from India or is composed of Indians. The truth by which it lives is that it is purely English.

This is most important; it must never be forgotten. The whole system of the government of India down to the last detail is alien, is exotic. It could not by any possibility be rooted in India. Neither the whole nor any part could be taken over as a going concern by any self-government India might develop. It was created by, and is adapted to, the genius of the English in India governing from above, and to that need only. The reader can see that for himself, and I beg that he will try to see it, because it is an essential truth.

Such was the principle of the English Government, one from above; and such were the people, a heterogeneous mass of diverse races, tongues and religions, with no organisation above that of the village.

That the people at large accepted our government as not only the best available government, but at the time the best conceivable government, there is no possible doubt. Nor, as I have said, was this acceptance merely passive. The ease with which Sepoy regiments were raised in all parts of India shows that the people had no antipathy to our government, but were glad to help it to restore and maintain order. For these troops were for internal purposes, and not for foreign service, which has always been most distasteful to them.

But there was more than this. The more you study governments and peoples the more clearly you see that to ensure smooth working there must be some relationship between them. Some emotion or some sentiment must unite the two, and so render their relative position endurable. Laws and restrictions are irksome; are never true; are negatives, not positives. There must be some tie between those who impose them and those who bear them to humanise them.

Now, there are two and only two systems of government that have ever been even partially successful anywhere in the world—one is self-government in such an organism as will allow the people not only to enforce their will but to form a right judgment as to what they should desire; the other is government by personality.

No complete form of either system has ever existed; the nearest to the former were the governments of Athens, Sparta, Rome in its early days, Venice, Florence, and some other self-governing cities. Instances of the latter are the temporary dictatorships of Rome, the rule of Alexander, Julius Caesar, Cromwell, Napoleon for the individual form; and the feudal system in England and the Continent for the aristocratic form. People in difficulties will trust personalities whom they admire and who have shown sympathy to them more than they will trust themselves, conscious that the former are more capable of seeing truly and of acting efficiently.

That which makes either of these systems of government a success is an emotion, a relationship.

With a really self-governing people this relationship is the sense of oneness between government and governed. However much the people may chafe under the laws and restrictions placed upon them they can console themselves with the idea that it is their own doing. Government is their own, part of themselves, and to that representative of self they can condone many things. Knowing it is their own, they realise that it does its best for them, however hard it may seem. They pardon because they can understand.

With an alien rule this sentiment cannot exist, and therefore another must take its place. That sentiment is personal feeling between the governed and the individual officers of government. Now that in India was very strong. For the soldiers and civilians who made India were personalities, and all people East and West admire strong personalities; moreover, they were sympathetic personalities who attracted confidence as well as admiration. District officers were the fathers of their district and stood up for their people against Law and Government.

The first secret of our success in India was the personality of our officers. Other things helped—the state of the country, the discipline of our English troops, the ability of the Home Government to help; but it was the personality of our officers that gave us India. Read all their records, right from Clive and Warren Hastings to Havelock, Lawrence and Nicholson. It was their personality that won. For personality alone can make bad laws bearable, can make mistakes forgiven and forgotten, can lead and draw men. And remember that it was not only the men at the top who were personalities, but all, right away down to the lowest ranks of both services. What personality is I do not know, but I know that it is the magic power of the world. It is the positive where all else in government is negative. I know it gave us India. I know that with the passing of personality there is coming the passing of the Empire. Read this story that has been given to me:

"An old General, who had served long in India, told me recently as follows: He still hears from time to time from his native subordinates in India. One of them wrote recently an account of his first meeting with the young official lately appointed to his station. As soon as was proper after the arrival of the official, the old Subadar went to pay his respects. He buckled on the sword which had descended to him from his father, took his father's medals in a packet in his hand, arrayed himself in his best uniform and called.

"After long delay he was introduced into the Presence, where he beheld a very untidy youth without coat or waistcoat busily writing at a table, surrounded by papers and stout books of reference.

"The great, tall, shy man modestly approached the table and laid his father's sword and his father's medals on it as a token of obeisance.

"After a while the scribe glanced up with angry and distracted expression, pushed all these tributes away disdainfully, and in a bitter voice complained of interruption.

"'Sir,' said the Subadar, 'these are the medals of my father who fought for you. This sword has been red with the blood of my own fellow-countrymen slain by my father in defence of your Raj, but as they do not interest you I will take them away.'"

So he went away.

But why blame the young civilian? He is as his teachers made him. I doubt not that he too once had a personality before his teachers killed it.

It is a common shibboleth amongst English writers on India that the "Oriental understands only personal government," and it is exactly the frame of mind that can invent such sayings that is the great stumbling-block to our understanding India. For neither in this nor in any other fundamental attitude does the East differ from the West. Look at England under Gladstone. There was again government by personality, and the country let him do things it would allow no one else to do. Nowadays in England the personality has gone on both sides, as well as self-government.

We gave India government by personality, that is to say, a government wherein alien laws, alien ideas, alien methods were rendered endurable by the medium through which they reached the people.

Therefore in the beginning, say from a hundred and fifty years ago till fifty years ago, the government and people were well suited to each other. In that time neither changed very greatly. Change there was, of course, but it was slow and slight. Then from the middle of the last century the rate of change was accelerated. Now life is change, and without change you can have only death; therefore there is nothing to regret in this. Had the change been in drawing more nearly together it would have been entirely fortunate. But it was not so. They were more nearly together in the beginning than ever since, and all progress has been away from each other. Instead of time bringing greater community of thought, greater mutual respect, and better understanding, with every year that passed, it widened and deepened the gulf between them. Instead of government becoming more suited to the people, it has grated on them more and more; instead of its efficiency increasing with the perfection of the machine, it has become less. In development, in intricacy, the government of to-day is to the government of a hundred years ago as a "Mauretania" to a "Great Eastern"; but whereas of old the wheels went easily, now they stick and try to stop; were there not a strong driving power behind them they would stop.

Let us see how this has occurred.

Yet before beginning to read this attempt to diagnose the state of the government of India and the paralysis that has come over it, I would ask the reader to remember this:

This book is not a mere criticism of government and its methods, nor of the people and their defects. I have a remedy to propose for both. It is a remedy that I have thought over and worked at for years, and I believe it is the only remedy possible.

But before disclosing it I wish the reader to understand the present state of things. If he retains the complacency which says that "all is for the best in the best of all possible governments, it is the people's fault entirely, visit it on them," then he will not realise that any remedy is wanting. Even if he do admit that something is wrong he will not know what it is, and cannot judge if that proposed be of any use.

Therefore I ask him to bear with the diagnosis of the earlier chapters. He must get to know first what the constitution of the government of India is, what made its strength in the past, and why that strength has departed from it. Only after a true diagnosis can a true cure be suggested. Therefore I ask him to carefully follow the line of thought in the chapters which show in what way government now fails. He will then see what government should be and must be—and is not. Only then can he judge if the proposed remedies are likely to be successful, and perhaps he will be able to amend them or to better them.

CHAPTER II
THE PEOPLE

Let us first take the people as a whole.

I am aware in the first place that there are some who will object that the Indian peoples are not a whole. "There is no Indian people," they will say. "There are innumerable races, tribes, castes, diffused over a continent. They have nothing in common, neither language nor religion, nor habits nor ideals. You cannot talk of the people as a whole."

Yet they have one thing in common; they have a common humanity. Religions, castes and races are but clothes. Beneath them lies humanity. And humanity is always the same in essence because it is one Soul striving towards one object, though in many different ways and in various stages of attainment.

I will show this by one instance. It is said, for example, that the instinctive feeling of an Oriental towards women is different from that of Europe; the West respects women, and the East does not do so. This is proved to you by their habits, by polygamy, by polyandry, by, for instance, the habit of a man walking in front and the woman behind. These customs, you are told, disclose the Oriental attitude as different from ours and as differing in various parts of the East.

They do not do so.

The instinctive feeling of men to women is the same everywhere; it is an invariable emotion. Customs hide it, disguise it, and sometimes almost kill it; they never alter it.

A Burman walks in front of his wife because in the very recent past, everywhere in Burma, and in most places even now, the advance was the place of difficulty. There were no roads, only paths through jungle or across the fields. There were thorny creepers to be cut back, streams and mud puddles to be forded, cattle and buffaloes to be driven away, snakes to be killed, and the nasty, snapping pariah dogs to be kept at a distance. No woman could or would go in front. The man goes in front from courtesy and carries a chopper, the woman follows with the bundle. It is their courtesy. If this habit continues when the necessity has passed, that is simply because a custom once established is, East or West, hard to break. See what Yoshio Markino says about this same custom in Japan.

Polyandry was due to restriction of the means of subsistence, limiting the population and so necessitating the exposure of girl children; occasional polygamy—for it is always only occasional, exceptional—is an imperfection of humanity, universal East or West. In the East they try to make the best of it by acknowledging it; the West hides it and pretends it does not exist. That is a difference of treatment, not of fact.

If you want to know the true instinctive feeling of men to women in the East you will find it not in laws, customs, or religions, but in the literature. Read their folk-tales, their love-stories, those which warm the hearts of boys and girls, of men and women, aye even of the old, those that rising from the heart appeal unto the heart. Their ideals are our ideals—one woman and one man; and I think sometimes they come nearer their realisation than we do. We pretend more, but pretence is not reality.

If this be true of love, the mother of all emotions, it is true of all the others. Their circumstances being different they must find different ways of reaching towards their ideals, but the ideals are the same.

Therefore all the Indian peoples have a common humanity; and more, they have a great many circumstances in common. They are all, for instance, mainly agricultural; they are all in a very similar stage of evolution—the village community stage; they are all poor, they are all natural and simple; they are all under our rule. These are more potent influences than religion or race if they are allowed to have their sway.

Then as to races, I do not think, for instance, that races in India are much more mixed than in Italy. Think of the races there are all grouped under the name Italian: there are Roman, Etruscan, Greek, Saracen, Norman, Goth—who shall say how many more? And in Great Britain I cannot count them.

Therefore, because in this book I am speaking of the real humanity hid beneath the clothes, the bonds, the chains of conventions and of customs, of religions and belief, I can speak of the Indian peoples as one people. Details differ enormously, but details do not ever affect principles, only the method of their application. And creeds, faiths, laws, and customs pass; humanity remains.

The Indian people, then, over whom we established our government accepted it, and helped us to establish it. They wanted peace. For two centuries or more they had been torn with wars, with insurrections, with internal anarchy, and with their consequences. They wanted rest, to plough, to sow, to reap, to trade in peace. We gave them that. They wanted Courts Criminal and Civil that were not corrupt. We gave them honest Judges. They wanted facilities for trade—roads, posts, and such things—which we provided. They could expand and use some of their energies.

But the field was a narrow one. Men are not born to sow and reap and trade alone. They have other emotions which seek for outlet, other energies which require a vent. Man is gregarious, and he is so made that he cannot fully develop himself except in larger and again larger communities. To reach his full stature in any way he must develop in all ways. He must feel himself part of ever greater organisms, the village first, the district and the nation—finally of humanity.

But in India all this is impossible. Except the village there is no community that exists even in name, and we have injured, almost destroyed, even that. Thus an Indian has no means of growth. He cannot be a citizen of anything at all. Half his sympathies and abilities lie entirely fallow, therefore he cannot fully develop the other half. A man is a complete organism, and if you keep half in inaction you affect the other half too. A man is not a worse but a better merchant, or lawyer, or landowner, or soldier, because he is interested in his locality, his community, his nation. It gives him wider views, makes him more tolerant, more humane, more wise. Man as a unit is a poor thing, physically, morally, and intellectually. Ability is the product of communities, of men formed into organisms, not of individuals. Each man in himself has no duty but to himself; to own a duty to a community he must be part of the community; to a government he must have a place in the government; to a nation he must be part of the nation. But in India there is no nation, no community at all, save very weakened village communities. As far as the Indian is concerned no larger community exists. And I have already pointed out that India has no place in the organism of government.

It is the slowly growing consciousness of an energy that has no outlet, of a desire for advance in every direction, that causes the unrest. In some ways the educated classes feel it most. Elsewhere they see men of their class cultivating their patriotism, increasing that sense of being and working for others, of being valuable to the world at large, showing capacity for leading, ruling, thinking, advancing in a thousand ways, while none of it is for them. They want to express the genius of their races in wider forms than mere individuality, but they are not able to do so. They want a national science and literature and law; they cannot have it. No individual as an individual can achieve anything. Not till he feels he is a cell in a greater and more enduring life can he develop. But this is not for India.

It is a piece of advice often addressed to India when she expresses her desire for some share in her government that she should first reform herself socially and intellectually. The status of women in zenanas and harems, infant marriage, the sad condition of widows, the degradation of caste, polygamy, the fanaticism of religions, are, she is told, to be mended before she can show herself fit for self-government in any form. Only to a free people can self-government be safely entrusted, and she is so wrapped up in prejudice and ignorance that she is unfit for any freedom. "Mend your divisions first; reform yourself, and we will see what we can do."

Such advice comes from ignorance alone. It is but another instance of that Phariseeism that has become so common with us. It is impossible for individuals to reform themselves, however much they may wish to do so. For an individual to reform, his whole environment must be reformed as well. For example, take widow remarriage. How can widows remarry in comfort till the whole structure of Hindu convention is changed? Not one individual nor a million individuals can break a convention. There is a strong feeling, as we know, amongst Hindus against this and many other conventions that stifle them, but every effort to break these chains has failed. Why? Because to break fetters bound upon society by religion or convention takes the combined effort of society, and even then it is difficult. The inertia of peoples is a deadly difficulty to overcome.

But we have not allowed the collective instinct any opportunity of developing.

There are no nuclei; there is nothing to draw the people together.

Take again the differences created by races, religions, castes. It is the interest of the priests to maintain these differences and exaggerate them. Religions never reform themselves. What influence is there to soften them? None that I ever heard of.

But self-governing institutions do tend to remove them. In the village communal life they are to a considerable extent ignored. The organism of the village, when healthy and free, forces men to disregard artificial barriers of this sort and meet on common ground for common business. Solidarity comes from the sense of the necessity for solidarity in order to get on. Its possibility is soon manifest.

But where in India is there any influence tending towards this end? The barriers of caste increase and grow, as naturally they must do. There is no *rapprochement* between Hindu and Mohammedan, but on the contrary the gulf is widened. It must be so. And if Government makes the fatal error of adopting the motto "*Divide et impera,*" if it in ever so slight a fashion identifies itself with one caste, race, or religion above another, then it is near the end of all things. But to the development of self-government the effacement of these divisions would be necessary, and in the pursuit of an eagerly coveted ideal they could pass and disappear. No other influence can do it. Again history shows this clearly. It was this influence in England that rendered Catholic emancipation possible and had brought creeds politically together. Did we in England live still under an aristocracy as we did a hundred years ago the divisions between Catholic and Protestant, Churchman and Dissenter, Christian and Agnostic, would still be as sharp as they were. These artificial barriers of creed and race give way only under the pressure of a stream of national life. That is beginning already to flow in India; be ours the task to help it flow in true and widening channels so that it may become a great river, fertilising all things. Now the main idea seems to be to dam it up, and so cause it to flood and to destroy.

I hope that what I say will not be misunderstood. I do not for a moment mean that political organisms should or could be used for social reform. That is quite impossible. Any such attempt would wreck the organism, which, as an organism, must pursue only its legitimate ends.

But I say, and all history is at one with me, that suitable free institutions do cultivate and bring out the faculty for freedom, and demonstrate that in all matters it is necessary.

Again, consider this: the laws concerning marriage, divorce, adoption, and inheritance, whether of Mohammedan, Hindu, or Buddhist, are petrified. With changing circumstances, changes in these laws become of the first necessity; yet as things are now no change is possible. Take the ten million Buddhists in Burma. Their laws of marriage are contained in the Dhammathats, which are derived from the laws of Menu, and are I don't know how old. Now there is this that is good about them: they were codified when India was free, before the night of religious bigotry descended upon it. They are, therefore, based not upon religious ideas, but upon custom which was based on experience. The spirit therefore is excellent, it is common-sense; it is not the pretension of an ideal long before the ideal is universally possible, but a common-sense recognition of human nature as it is, and the necessity of doing your best with it. They are the only marriage laws in the world framed by common sense and not religion. Men and women are free and equal. But although their base is excellent they were framed for a very different environment from what obtains now. And again, there are two or more codes, and they differ in details. There is nothing the people want more than a rectification and consolidation of their laws, with registration of marriage, the power to make wills, and other matters. They are always expressing this necessity because the present laws of inheritance handicap them against other races. They cannot make wills, and the law of inheritance is so vague that when a rich man dies litigation almost always ensues. The estate is dissipated in law-costs and the heirs ruined.

But who is going to draft the new laws? Not Government. Once bit twice shy, and the Government of Madras had a try at that in Malabar. There was urgent necessity there for some system of marriage registration, so Government appointed a Commission which recorded quantities of evidence, and framed a Report, on which an Act was passed. It was supposed to be absolutely according to the wishes of the people. I have not been in Malabar since the Act was passed, but one friend has told me that three marriages were registered under it. Another friend told me that this is a wild exaggeration, and that only one marriage was registered under it, just that the people might say they had not rejected the Act without trying it. However this may be, the Act is a dead letter. It was bound to fail. The people find the laws of Government already too stringent, interfering too much, and too inhuman, even where they deal with matters outside the home. They will never allow an alien Government a footing inside the house. They know Government has destroyed the village; they fear it will destroy the family. Therefore Government holds its hand. It cannot do otherwise. For even if it could frame an Act in accordance with the wishes of the people, that Act could not be enforced. And it cannot discover the wishes of the people, because the people themselves don't know. The opinion of no matter how many individuals is no true guide. Because, to justify a new Act of inheritance, not individual opinion but joint opinion must be known. They are not the same. Ten men as individuals will tell you one thing; these ten men as a community would tell you a different thing. This is a fact in psychology I shall have to refer to again later. It is undoubted.

Now the joint opinion of Burmese society as to the proposed change cannot be gauged, because it does not exist. There are no Burmese communities to evolve any common idea. Therefore the archaic laws must remain as they are.

Thus throughout India all progress of all sorts is barred; can you wonder that there is unrest from this one cause alone?

And this feeling goes down to the very lowest ranks as an unnameable, unanalysable fever and unhappiness; you see it everywhere.

Then there is more than this. A system of government and law that was bearable when we were weak is unbearable when stronger. What gives you help when young becomes a fetter as you grow. It bites into the flesh like cords too tightly drawn, and in India instead of being loosed they have been drawn more tightly year by year.

It is not only that the people have grown bigger, but the bonds of government have grown narrower. It has grown more of a machine, less human than it was, less human year by year, until sometimes now it is almost inhuman in its rigid formalism. The bonds cut into her flesh; India wants to grow, to rise—but cannot. How could it be but that she should show unrest?

India wants to get on; we bar the way, so India feels unrest.

Now if you will consider this unrest you will admit that it is not a bad symptom but a good one; it is a sign of an increasing life. Neither is it uncomplimentary to us that it should have arisen. It is the greatest compliment our rule could have. A hundred and fifty years ago—even, perhaps, fifty years ago—India could not have felt this. She was exhausted, weary, wanting peace. We gave her peace, and so she has grown strong and overcome her weariness. That is our doing. No one else could have done that. We gave her a complete rest cure. We said, "Keep still, and eat and drink; we will do all the thinking—the ruling that has to be done. Do not be afraid, for we can do it well. Have confidence. Get back your nerves and strength. We will look after you."

We did. How well we did it history tells. We did not spare ourselves. I do not say we acted from any altruistic motives. I do not say we have not made mistakes. But we did it. The task was great; the greatest, perhaps, the world has seen.

India is rested, and she wakes, she moves. Why are we angry? Should we not feel proud?

Can we not give her a hand, and say, "Rise up and try to walk. I will hold your hand at first, till you are stronger. Then when you are grown you shall walk free, beside me, as my daughter whom I have brought up"?

I see continual denunciations of the unrest in India. Why? I see continual regrets that the past is passed—but why? Continual threats are breathed towards India. Why?

For myself, I hail it as the happiest omen that could be. It has unfortunate exhibitions sometimes; that is partly our fault, I fear, because we do not recognise that the past is gone for ever. India has grown, and we forget. We give no outlet to these true energies that have developed. India was our patient; now she is recovering shall we make of her a subject, or a daughter? She must be one or other, or leave us altogether, for the past is passed.

CHAPTER III

THE CIVILIAN

Let us now consider the Government and its ideas; that is to say, the men and the laws by which they govern.

First, take the *personnel,* for there is no complaint more insistent on all sides than that the officers of to-day are not the same as those of fifty or more years ago. They are out of touch with the people.

It was for some time supposed by Government that this was only partially true. That government itself, that is, the Secretariats, was out of touch, was felt and avowed. But it was supposed that this arose from the specialising of function. The work of secretaries had become so difficult, so special, so different from district work, that instead of there being interchange of officers, the secretaries usually passed all their official lives away from actual contact with the realities of the people. There were orders passed that in future this was not to occur, men were to come and go, to do district work for a while, and then secretariat work, bringing to the latter knowledge gained in the former.

But it was quickly seen that this had little or no result. If the secretaries were out of touch, the district officers were hardly less so. Government, as a whole, had separated from the people. English and Indian were divided; nothing was gained.

What, then, was the difference between the men of the past and those of the present? Let us consider.

They went out younger in those days; sixteen, seventeen, or eighteen, were the usual ages. The usual age for Haileybury cadets was twenty. Clive, Warren Hastings, Nicholson and John Lawrence went out at eighteen, Henry Lawrence at seventeen, Meadows Taylor at fifteen. Many of the administrators were soldiers first, and they too went out young. Lord Roberts, for instance, landed in India when he was sixteen. Addiscombe cadets joined at sixteen or seventeen. When Haileybury was abolished the average age was raised to twenty-three or more, and at that age it now remains.

Thus, as the first year in India is also spent in training out there, a man is now not far from twenty-five before he is allowed to act independently; he used to be twenty-one or less. This is a great difference.

In England the age when a boy attains his majority and has full freedom before the law is twenty-one, and in order to elucidate this question I have tried to discover why the law of England fixed twenty-one. In Rome a boy was legally of age as regards his person at fourteen though he had a curator over his property till he was twenty-five. Therefore this age of twenty-one does not come from Roman law. It seems to have arisen from a general consensus of observation that at twenty-one the average young man is fit to be free and should be free. There seems to be about that age a critical mental stage of adolescence corresponding to the physical stage at fourteen. However this may be, there seems to be no doubt that to keep a young man in tutelage till he is twenty-four or twenty-five is bad for him. The powers of initiative and the sense of responsibility which mature at twenty-one atrophy thereafter if not fully used. And no book learning can replace this. Thus nowadays tutelage is too long continued.

Again, education began later in those days than now, and there was less of it. Boys ran wild far more than now, when they are cramped up in schools and conventions at a very early age.

Thus the men of old had individualities; they had not been steam-rollered flat by public school and university; their boyish enthusiasm and friendliness were still in them. They had no prejudices, had never heard of the Oriental mind, were not convinced beforehand that every Oriental was a liar and a thief, but were prepared to take men as they found them. They were willing and eager to learn. Their minds were open as yet to new impressions. They had not been "fortified by fixed principles" to "safeguard them" against acquiring any sympathy with Eastern peoples. Therefore they did so understand and sympathise.

If you will read the records of the past you will see this in a most marked degree. Englishmen had Indian friends; how rarely do they have such now! They knew the people's talk, their folk-lore and their tales. They looked on them as fellow-humans. And the feeling was reciprocated. Look, for instance, at how they kept the same servants all their service. Nowadays there is a general howl of the badness of Indian servants and their untrustworthiness. It was not so then. One of the most pleasing features of that old life was the affection often shown between masters and servants. Dickens has noted it. How much of that do you find now? Not much. A little still there is—who should know better than I? And if now it is so rare, where is the fault? Good masters make good servants. And it requires so little goodness in the master—only a little consideration, a friendly word sometimes. They give back far more than they receive. If there are many bad servants, who makes them bad? Their masters; those with whom they began their service, who did not know how to treat them, how to help them, how to keep them. At Arcot the Sepoys gave the rice to their officers and took the conjee themselves; how many regiments would do that now?

I do not say that there was ever close personal intercourse between English and Indian; there was not, and in the nature of things there could not be. But there were mutual consideration and mutual respect. "We have different ways and different customs; we have different skins. But underneath it all we are both men." So they thought in the old days.

Thus in the old days the embryo official came out young, free from prejudices, full of enthusiasms, ready to learn, to read, to mark, learn, and inwardly digest all phases of Oriental life about him. Even thirty years ago when I first went to India there were many of this type still left. They thought it their duty, as it was their pleasure, to study the people in order to understand what lay beneath their customs. It must be thirty years ago that an old civilian turned on me sharply when I made some ignorant remark about some Malabar custom and said: "The custom has arisen out of the circumstances of life and no peculiarity of nature in the people. All peoples are much alike in fundamentals, and great apparent differences are but superficial, and arise from environment."

The absurd doctrine of the "Oriental mind" had not then arisen to be an excuse for ignorance and want of understanding. Nowadays it is supposed to be the mark of culture to talk of it; to the old officials it would have been the mark of a fool; they thought it their duty to study the people.

But it is not so now. Young civilians come out with their minds already closed, and, as a rule, closed they remain. The harm is done in England before they start. Let me give instances.

It is a custom when a young civilian joins to send him to a district head-quarters for six months first, to learn his way about before posting him to any specified work. One such was sent to me ten years ago, and if I give an account of him it will do for all. For nowadays they are all turned out of the same mill, have all the same habits of mind and thought, and their personalities are submerged. If anything, he of whom I speak was above the average in all ways.

He was a very nice young fellow, with charming manners, and I greatly liked him.

He became an officer of great promise, and would have risen high, but he is dead now, and therefore what I say now cannot offend anyone. Besides, I have nothing to say that would offend. He was, I think, twenty-three years of age, of good people, educated at a public school and Oxford, and was as nice a boy as could be found. He had passed high in the examinations. He was said to be clever, and as regards assimilating paper knowledge, he was able, but his mind was an old curiosity shop. He had fixed ideas in nearly everything. He was full of prejudices he called principles, of "facts" that were not true. He had learnt a great deal, he knew nothing; and worse—he did not know how to obtain knowledge. He wanted his opinions ready-made and absolute first, and only sought for such facts as would support those principles. He had no notion how to make knowledge by himself. He wanted authority before he would think. Give him "authority," and he would disregard or deny fact in order to cling to it. I will take a concrete instance.

There is amongst Englishmen in Burma a superstition that the Burmese do not and cannot work. They are "lazy." The men never work if they can help it, and all the work that is done is done by women. How this idea arose is an interesting study in the psychology of ignorance, but I need not enter into that now. The idea obtains universally, and is an acknowledged shibboleth. My young assistant was not with me many days before he brought it up.

"Oh," he said, "the Burman is so lazy."

"You are sure of that?" I asked.

He stared at me. "Why, everyone says so."

"Everyone said four hundred years ago that the sun went round the earth," I answered; "were they right?"

"You don't mean to tell me," he said, "that the Burmese can work."

"I don't mean to tell you anything," I answered. "Here are a quarter of a million Burmese in this district. Find out the facts for yourself."

The necessity of having to support his theories with facts seemed to him unreasonable. "But," he objected, "I can see they are lazy." The Burman is lazy. That is enough said. What have facts to do with it? He did not say this, but undoubtedly he was thinking it. However, at last he did find what he considered a fact.

"You remember, when we rode into that village the other day about noon, the number of men we saw sleeping in the veranda?"

"True," I said.

"Does not that show it?"

"Suppose," I said, "you had got up at four o'clock in the morning and worked till ten, in the fields, would you not require a rest before going out at three o'clock again?"

"Do they do that?" he asked.

"You can find out for yourself if they do or not," I answered.

He looked at me doubtfully.

"But," he objected, "it is notorious."

"So is the fact that the standard of living in Burma is very high. How do you reconcile the two? Laziness and comfort. The comfort is evident and real, perhaps the laziness is only apparent."

"A rich country," he said.

"Is it?" I asked. "Look at the dry, bare land, of which nearly all this district and most of Upper Burma are composed. Is it rich? You have eyes to see. You know it is not rich; why do you say it is?"

He shook his head almost as if I had hurt him and searched about for a defence.

"But Lower Burma is rich."

"Certainly; and if you look at the export returns you will see the enormous amount of rice it grows and exports. Is that rice the product of laziness?"

"But," he said at last in despair, "if this laziness of the Burman is untrue, how did the idea become general?"

"Ah," I answered, "that is another matter. Let us stick to one thing at a time. We are concerned now with whether it is true or not. Decide that first. See for yourself. Find out an ordinary man's work and I think you will find it is sufficient.

You have the opportunity of judging, and unless you use that opportunity you have no right to an opinion at all."

He said no more at the time, but a few days later he returned to the subject. A High Official had been opening a public work in Mandalay and had made a speech. Much of the labour for the work had been Burmese, where usually such labour is imported Indian, and he referred with satisfaction to the fact. "I am glad to see," said the High Official, "that the Burmese are taking to hard work." My assistant brought this up. "Here is authority," he said.

"Certainly," I said; "there is authority on one side; now let us look at fact on the other; whether is it better to be a peasant-proprietor on your own land or a day-labourer?"

"The proprietor, of course," he said.

"This has been a bad year in some districts. Crops have failed. You can read that from the weekly reports in my office. Many cultivators have had to abandon their holdings and turn to day labour. Is that good? Are they to be congratulated on it?"

The boy looked downcast.

"No," he admitted.

"Well, then," I asked, "what will they think of a Government who says such things?"

He reflected for some time. "But," he said at length, "when one authority (the High Official) says one thing and another authority (you) says the reverse, what am I to believe?"

Then came my opportunity. "You are to believe nothing," I said. "You have eyes, you have ears, you have common sense. They are given you to use and see facts for yourself. The facts are all round you. You will never do any good work if you refuse to face facts and understand them. If you are to be worth your salt as an official you will have to work by sight, not by faith."

He laughed. At first he seemed puzzled; then he was pleased. He had been educated to accept what he was told and never to question. His mind had been stunted and the idea of exercising it again delighted him. To judge by himself was a new idea to him entirely and he welcomed it. He began to do so. For the first time since childhood he was encouraged to use that which is the only thing worth cultivating—his common sense. But even yet he could not emancipate himself.

Some time later a new subject came up. This time it was the disappearance of the Burman. He is supposed to be dying out. The Indian is "ousting" him. Before long there will be none left. My assistant had read it in the paper and heard it almost universally, therefore it must be true. I said nothing at the time, but that day when I went to office I sent him the volumes of the last two Census tables with a short note. "Will you kindly," I wrote, "make out for me:

the Burmese population in 1891
the Burmese population in 1901

district by district, and let me know where there have been decreases, also increases, and the percentage of increase."

The next day he came to me with an amused expression on his face and a paper of figures in his hand.

"I have made them all out," he said, "as you wished. Here they are."

"Then," I said, "let us take the districts with the decreases first. Please show me them."

"There are none," he answered. "They all show increases."

"Large?" I asked.

"Yes, large," he said; "from a population of about nine million to ten million in ten years is a good increase. The Burmese are prolific."

"But," I remarked also, "I thought the Burman was disappearing? You said so on authority. How is that?"

He laughed; he had taken his lesson.

And again, another point. I had received an order from Government which I thought was mistaken, and I said so. He was a Government official too, and I could say to him what I could not say to others.

"Then you won't carry it out?" he asked, surprised.

"I am here to carry out orders," I answered, "and of course I shall carry it out."

"But why then do you criticise it, if it must be carried out?"

"Look here," I said, "before very long you will be sent to a subdivision of my district to govern it. I shall send you many orders, and shall expect you to carry them out."

"Right or wrong?"

"Right or—as you may think—wrong. You must do as I say. Without this, government is impossible. But I do not want you to think as I do. I want you to think for yourself. If an order appears to you issued from a misconception on my part, you must not refuse to obey; but I should expect you to tell me any facts that would lead me to better knowledge. Your business is not merely to carry out orders, but to furnish me with correct information how to better those orders. You are not merely to be part of the district hand, but of its brain too. I should want you to criticise every order in your mind, try to understand it, and if you disagree with it to examine your reasons for disagreement and see if they are good."

"And let you know?"

"Whenever you are certain that I am wrong, and the matter is important."

"But would not criticism be cheek?"

"Not if it is true and valuable. You would be doing me a valuable service. It is what I want. How do you suppose we are ever to get on if opinions are to be stereotyped? Thought must be free. But don't give me opinions or 'authority.' I don't care for either. Give me facts, and be sure of your facts."

"I see," he said.

"You can be quite kind about it, you know," I suggested.

"Is that what you are to Government," he asked, "when you disagree with them?"

"I try to be," I said. "I put myself as far as I can in their position, and give them what I would like to receive myself."

Again it was quite a new idea to him that anyone should want criticism. He had been educated to believe that any doubt of what authority said was a sin, perhaps inevitable sometimes, but anyhow always to be concealed; and he had been told that everyone, from the Creator down, resented criticisms and would annihilate the critic. That anyone should prefer knowing the truth even if it prove him wrong seemed to him impossible. He did not like ever to admit he had been wrong. He thought truth was absolute and fixed, whereas it is relative and always growing. He had, unconsciously, the mind of the Pharisee in the Temple.

Now these three instances will point out what seems to me to be wrong in the previous training of young men sent to India, and in fact in all training. Their minds instead of being cultivated are stifled. They are taught to disregard fact and to accept authority in place of it. They are not only to do what they are told, which is right; but to think what they are told, which is wrong. And they do. They are taught to repeat in parrot manner stock phrases and imagine they are thinking. And this habit once acquired is difficult to get rid of. With most it never is got rid of. You will, for instance, find these shibboleths of the "disappearing Burman" and his "laziness" repeated by the highest officials who have been longest in the country, all of whom have facts in their office disproving them. And these are not the only prejudices nor even the principal. They are innumerable and serious. You will in consequence find that administration and even legislation are affected by them. The whole attitude of Government to the people it governs is vitiated in this way. There is a want of knowledge and understanding. In place of it are fixed opinions based usually on prejudice or on faulty observation, or on circumstances which have changed, and they are never corrected. Young secretaries read up back circulars, and repeat their errors indefinitely. That is "following precedent." They will quote you complacently:

"Freedom broadening slowly down
From precedent to precedent"

and never see the absurdity of the lines. Freedom is the disregard of precedent where the precedent is wrong or out of date.

There is throughout nearly all English officials (and non-officials) in India not only a disregard of facts about them, but a want of any real sympathy with the people among whom they live, which is astonishing. They often like the "natives," they often are kind to them, wish them well, and do their best for them, but that is not sympathy. Sympathy is understanding. It is being able to put yourself in another's place.

I could tell many stories illustrating this want of understanding. One will suffice. An official I knew well, an excellent fellow, kind-hearted, humorous, and able, holding a good position then and a high one now, with a charming wife, living amongst the Burmese and ruling them, with Burmese servants, clerks, and peons, and continual Burmese visitors of all classes, called his dog "Alaung." Now "Alaung" means something very similar to "Messiah," and is a sacred word. A parallel would be if, say, a Parsee in England called his dog "Christ." I have seen this official's servants wince when he called out to his dog. Yet I am sure it never struck him that there was anything out of the way in this nomenclature. I am sure he never dreamed he would hurt anyone's feelings by it, or he would not have done it. He certainly intended no jeer at the religion of his subordinates. It was simply that he wanted understanding.

Now sympathy is inherent in all children, and is the means whereby they acquire all the real knowledge they have. A girl being a mother to her doll, a boy being a soldier or hunter, is exercising and training the most valuable of all gifts—imaginative sympathy. It is the only emotion which brings real knowledge of the world about you. Without it you never understand anything.

It should be incessantly cultivated and fed with real facts to enable it to grow, and to turn what your sympathy leads you to suspect into what knowledge confirms. In all young men nowadays it is destroyed by their education. Their minds are fitted up with obsolete and mistaken prejudices, which are called principles, and then the door is locked. They all talk the same, act the same, have the same ideas in their heads. None of them ever think over what is all about them. They do their work by paper knowledge and paper principles; the great book of humanity has been sealed for them. When they try to think they cannot do so. They have lost the power their childhood had. They argue in the most extraordinary way. They will make a statement, and if it is disproved say, "Well, if it is not true it ought to be," and go on as if that made it true. They will resort to prophecy, and say, "If not true to-day it will be to-morrow," and so settle it.

Now if brighter days are to be in store for India official or non-official, English or native, all this must be altered. The whole principles of education must be revised or abandoned. The less educated a man is now the more real understanding he is likely to have. The educated man is a mental automaton. He has sold his soul and got in its place some maxims, with the aid of which he seeks to govern the world. He thinks knowledge is got from books. It is not. Books are most valuable helps, showing you new views of life, giving you new facts, showing you how to think; but they never give you knowledge of life. Only experience can do that. But the young man now does not want to know what is, but what other people say. He is afraid of himself and yearns for authority.

This has been evident to all who have looked into the matter. Here is what a modern writer says:

"No English schoolboy is ever taught to speak the truth for the very simple reason that he is never taught to desire the truth. From the very first he is taught to be totally careless as to whether a fact is a fact; he is taught to care only whether the 'fact' can be used on his side when he is engaged in 'playing the game.'"

Nothing could be more true than this. He is provided with fixed ideas, and he will welcome any fact that supports them, while deliberately refusing all facts which are opposed to his ideas. He thinks and argues to prove his preconceived point, never to elicit truth regardless of whether that truth agrees with his preconceptions or not. In fact, he is taught not to think. The Inward Light which is in all children has been put out. He has become a spiritual coward; he dare not look the whole truth in the face. He thinks that patriotism consists in supporting his country or his class through thick and thin. It does not occur to him that the higher patriotism is to try to help his country or his class not to go wrong, or if wrong to get right. He would rather bolster up a mistake, shut his eyes to the fact that it is a mistake, and go on doing it, than admit his wrong. It is better in his eyes to be consistently wrong than by admitting mistakes and correcting them to be inconsistent. He cannot learn.

CHAPTER IV

HIS SUBSEQUENT TRAINING

Therefore there is a wide difference between the men as they came out in the old days and as they come out now. Then they were young, not very well instructed but capable of seeing, understanding, and learning; nowadays they are so drilled and instructed that they can deal only with books, papers, and records; life has been closed to them; they can enforce laws, but not temper them.

After they come out the difference of life and work is still greater. In the old days, for instance, they picked up the language quickly and well. The time to learn a language is when you are young—the younger the better. We learn our own language as children. The older we grow the harder it is, because it means not merely learning by heart a great many words, not merely training the palate and tongue to produce different sounds, but adopting a new attitude of mind. Nothing definite has been discovered as to the localisation of faculties in the brain, therefore nothing certain is known; but it has always seemed to me and to others whom I have consulted that when you learn a new language you are exercising and developing a new piece of brain. When you know several languages and change from one to another you seem definitely to change the piece of brain which actuates your tongue. You switch off one centre and switch on to another. You will always notice in yourself and others that there is a definite pause when the change of language is made. Now it becomes every year more difficult to awaken an unused part of the brain and bring it into active use, and to begin at twenty-three is late. True, languages are taught them at Oxford before they come out, but the result seems *nil*. You must learn a language where it is spoken. Moreover, the way they have been taught Latin and Greek is a hindrance, for living languages are not learnt that way. A child, for instance, learns to talk perfectly without ever learning grammar. I never heard that any great English writer had a grounding in English grammar. There is no real grammar of a living language, because it grows and changes. You can only have a fixed grammar of a dead language.

The fact is that correct talking is the outcome of correct thinking, not of any mechanical rules. You must think in a language before you can speak it well.

But at twenty-three it is far too late for the ordinary man to learn to think in Hindustani or Burmese or Tamil. Of course there are occasional exceptions, but the way these languages are usually spoken is dreadful. I could tell tales about myself as well as others, for though I worked very hard for years I never knew Burmese well, nor yet Canarese, nor yet Hindustani. Yet who will doubt that it is very important, the most important acquisition, in fact, that you can make? Without it you can never really get near the people. So that in this way the old civilian had again a great advantage.

Here is one story. Once upon a time there was a District Officer and there was his district, and for some reason they did not seem to agree. At least the district did not like its Head. It felt uneasy, and it became restive, and at last it complained. It took up many grievances, and amongst them was this: "There is a good deal of building wanted in various parts, and there is timber and there are sawyers, but no licences can be obtained. When the Head comes round on tour we ask him, but he always refuses. So all building work is stopped."

An Inspecting Officer went to inquire, and he began with this complaint: "Why do you refuse them sawpit licences when on tour?" he asked.

"I don't," the Head replied.

"They say you do."

"But they never even applied; so how could I refuse?" he answered.

"Very well," said the Inspecting Officer, "let's see the file of your petitions received."

A clerk brought it out, and there—written in Burmese, of course—were many sawpit applications, and below each, written by the Head, was his endorsement:

"I cannot allow more guns to be issued."

Then the machine of government was far less perfected than it is now. There were, of course, laws and rules and there was supervision, but to nothing like the present extent. The district officer then had a personality. He was required to have one, for local conditions differed more than they do now and he had far more latitude. Moreover, the machine being less effective he depended a great deal upon his personal influence to keep the place quiet and get things done. He could not ask for orders because there was no telegraph, and he could not get help quickly because there were no railways. Therefore he was obliged to acquire a personal knowledge of people and peoples, of individuals and castes and races, which, he thinks, is not so necessary now. The result was that all laws and orders passed through his personality before reaching the people, thus acquiring a humanity and reasonableness that is now impossible. He studied his district and he used his powers, legal and otherwise, as he found best. If he found a law harsh—and in the last resort all laws are so—he would ameliorate its action. Nowadays he cannot do that. In the old days he administered, as best he could, justice; now he administers law—a very wide difference. Thus he was forced by circumstances to acquire a knowledge and a sympathy which are unattainable to-day; for you only learn things by doing them.

The old district officers were known personally by name and by reputation all through their districts. The people looked to them for help and understanding, and protection as much against the rigidity and injustice of the laws as against other ills.

But nowadays, except the Government officials and headmen, I don't believe anyone in a district knows who the head is. At all events, it makes practically no difference, because the application of the laws is supervised and enforced, and the district officer must "fall into line." If any personality has survived his schooling it must now be killed.

Few men, I think, learn anything except from two motives—a natural driving desire or necessity. But a natural desire to study the people round you is scarce, and the necessity of other days has passed away. A district officer can now do his work quite to the satisfaction of Government and know next to nothing of the people. In fact, sometimes knowledge leads to remonstrance with Government, and it doesn't like that.

Again, there has crept into secretariats a cult of "energy" and "efficiency," and a definition of these words, which acts disastrously upon the district officer, both when he is under training and subsequently.

Now, the proper meaning of an "efficient officer" is, I take it, one who sees the right thing to do and does it quickly and effectively; and probably Government really has this in its mind when it uses the word. This is what it wants; but very often what it gets is almost the opposite, and it is as pleased with this as if it got what it expected. In fact, it does not seem to know the difference. An example will explain what I mean.

There is, we will say, in a district a good deal of cattle theft going on, and the thieves cannot be detected. Cattle graze in Burma in the fields, and in the jungle on their outskirts; they roam about a good deal, and it is easy enough to steal them; detection is difficult.

But there is in Burma, as in parts of India, a provision of the Village Regulation which is called the Track Law, and it is substantially as follows:

> If cattle are missing their tracks can be followed. When they pass out of the area under the jurisdiction of the village wherein the owner lives and enter another village lands, that village becomes responsible. The tracker calls the headman of that village and shows him the tracks, which he must follow up and demonstrate that they have not stopped in his jurisdiction but gone on. In this way the tracks can be followed till they are lost, when the village in whose land they are lost is considered as being the village of the thief, and is therefore responsible for the lost cattle. It can be fined, and the owner of the lost bullock indemnified.

This Act is taken from a very old custom common once in most of India, and also, I believe, in places of Europe. For several hundred years ago, when villages were widely separated by jungle, it had some sense.

There was then a presumption either that the stolen bullock had been taken to that village, or that some of the villagers had seen it pass. The thief would probably have stopped there for food or rest, as it was a long way on. But nowadays, in most of the country, village fields are conterminous, with little or no jungle between; there are many roads, and except where the tracks actually go into the village gate the presumption does not arise. Cattle are common, and the villagers are not expert trackers. Moreover, there is a very strong premium on dishonesty, or at least carelessness in keeping to the right tracks. Suppose the right track lost in a wet place, or a dry bare place, why not pick up some other? Most cattle tracks are very similar. The owner wants his compensation.

Yet the "energetic" officer will be expected to work this Act *à pied de la lettre*.

I saw a good deal of the actual working of this Act at one time, when I was a subordinate officer. Every time a beast was lost it had to be tracked, and the village where the tracks were lost had to pay. It made no difference if there was any reasonable presumption against the village, there the law was. The tracks might be lost two miles from the actual village, simply crossing its boundary; the law was there.

I remember one village had a bad time because it was near a frequented road, and when the tracks got on this road they were always lost, as the surface was hard. So the village had to pay. Yet what evidence was there against the village? None. I had the curiosity for some time, whenever a case wherein a village was fined was subsequently detected, to find out what village had been fined, and see if that village had been in any way cognisant of the theft. It never had. The fine was purely gratuitous, was worse than useless, for it was wrong.

Yet it is a Government rule—not, I think, actually laid down, but understood—that whenever an offence occurs, unless the culprit is arrested a village must be held responsible.

I always disliked the Track Law and its subsidiary sections, not because I have any objection to holding a village, in certain cases, responsible for its members—I think it is a sound principle—but because it always hit innocent people, as far as I could see. I used it as little as I could, yet there were difficulties. I will mention a case in point.

There was a broker who lived not in my district but near its boundary, and one day he rode to a village in my district to collect some debts. He didn't collect them, and left the village in a rage, saying he would complain to the police-station six or seven miles away that he had been cheated. It was about four o'clock in the afternoon when he left, and he rode off across the plain in the direction of the police-station.

He was sighted at dusk near the river, going along a road which half a mile farther on passed through a village, and no more was seen of him. He never arrived at the police-station, and next morning his pony was found roaming the plain about the village near which he had last been seen.

There was no sign of him or his body.

He was a well-known man, reputed to be wealthy, and a great fuss was made. His wife declared he must have been murdered. The magistrate of the broker's district was indignant that "his" broker should have been murdered in my district and I do nothing. My police could get no clue at all, nor could I. A subordinate magistrate held a proceeding under the Track Law against the village where the broker disappeared, and recommended it be fined. I, however, held my hand.

Then a body was found floating in the river some miles lower down, and identified as the broker's body, and his wife gave it a funeral. Still I held my hand.

My neighbour was indignant; my Superintendent of Police was distressed at me; my Commissioner evidently thought me slack—"no energy." The fact is I was puzzled, and would do nothing till I saw clearly. So six months went on.

What would have happened eventually had nothing more come out I can't say, but something more did come out—the broker came out. He was recognised in Mandalay and immediately arrested—for pretending to be alive when he was really dead, I suppose—and sent to me. I asked him what had occurred, and he confessed that he was deeply in debt to money-lenders and had made up this scheme to defeat them. He had left his pony, gone down to the river, crossed in a canoe, and gone into hiding. While he was "dead" his wife had compounded with his creditors.

I sent him back to my neighbour with the emphatic warning that if his broker ever came up my way again he would certainly be done for in good earnest. The whole district had been turned upside down for him, and he was not popular.

Now the points that I wish all this to illustrate are these: Men at the head-quarters of Government, out of touch with real life, read the Track Law, think it most useful and just, and insist on its being enforced. Officers on the spot, accustomed to accept all law as the epitome of justice, follow the Act without thinking. The responsibility is really on them, as Government tells them to judge each case on its merits, but they fear that if they reported that no case under the Track Law ever had any merits they would be written down as "wanting in energy." As they have not been trained to think for themselves, they do not do so. They fulfil all the requirements of the Act, and are satisfied. Moreover, subsequently, to justify their own action they must praise the Act. Therefore a vicious circle is created. Government says: "District officers praise the Act, therefore have it stringently enforced, for they know its actual value." And district officers say: "Government declares this to be an admirable Act, therefore I must enforce it." No one ever investigates the facts. If a district officer have doubts, he discreetly smothers them as babies, lest they grow.

And this is but one instance. I mention in a later chapter a still more striking case of this sort of action; and even many examples would not expose its whole evil. It is the spirit that renders such things possible that is disastrous. So are officers trained to believe that when anything untoward happens they must do something—they must punish somebody. The idea that if they act without full knowledge the something they do will be wrong and the persons they punish will be innocent is not allowed to intrude. They will, of course, always act by law, but then, "*summum jus, summa injuria.*" In the old days this could not have happened. In the first place, Government trusted its officers, and its trust was not misplaced; now it trusts its laws; yet there is nothing so unintelligent, nothing so fatal as rigid laws—except those who believe in them. In the second place, officers with the personality and knowledge of the men of former days would have insisted on seeing for themselves and judging for themselves. They would have cared nothing that they might be supposed not to have "energy." They would know they had something better than that—they had understanding.

The possibility of making our laws and our government generally endurable to the people depends on the personality of the district officer.

Nowadays he is sent out with his personality crushed, and it gets still more crushed out there. He becomes in time not a living soul but a motor-engine to drive a machine. Whatever knowledge he acquires is of the people's faults and not their virtues. When you hear an official praised as "knowing the Indian" or "the Burman," you know that it means that he knows his faults. He knows the criminal trying to escape, the villager trying to evade revenue. It doesn't mean that he knows more than this. Some do, especially among the police and the forest officers, but then they have no influence.

As showing the difference between the old officer and the new I make the following extract from *A City of Sunshine*, by Alexander Allardyce. Few books on the East have been written with a clearer understanding.

"Mr. Eversley, the collector, was an official of a type that has almost passed away. He had been brought up in the strictest traditions of the Haileybury school and had adhered all his life to the conservative principles of the 'old civilianism.' When the 'Competition Wallah' came in, Eversley foresaw certain ruin to the English interests in India. 'Competition Wallahs!' he used to exclaim—'as well put the country under a commission of schoolmasters at once. But we'll lose the country with all this Latin and Greek; take my word for it we'll soon lose the country.' Mr. Eversley had never been able to make a hexameter in the whole course of his life, and there is grave reason to doubt that he was ignorant of even the barest elements of the Greek accidence. But he had acquired a marvellous colloquial familiarity with the Eastern vernaculars, and he knew the habits and feelings of the Bengalee better than any other officer in the Lower Provinces. There was no chance of Eversley falling into such a blunder as that which was laid to the charge of Muffington Prigge, the magistrate of the neighbouring district of Lallkor, who once, in taking the deposition of a witness in a criminal case, had expressed his displeasure that evidence of such importance should be given on the authority of a third person, and ordered the police to bring 'Fidwi' before him. The witness gave his evidence in the third person out of respect. Instead of saying 'I saw' he said 'Fidwi (your slave) saw.' Muffington Prigge's judgments had been more than once spoken of with encomiums by Mr. Justice Tremer in the Appeal side of the High Court, but Mr. Eversley's law never came before the High Court except to be reprobated. Lawyers complained that he did not know even the rudiments of the Codes; but there was no magistrate in the Lower Provinces whose decisions were received with more general satisfaction or from whose judgments there were fewer appeals. His rough-and-ready way of settling cases was better relished than the elaborate findings of the Lallkor archon which were generally unintelligible to the suitors till they had fee'd their lawyer to tell them which side had won.

"The people knew that Eversley would do what he saw to be right, independent of Act or Code, *and they had more confidence in his sense of justice than in the written law.*"

What is the highest praise a Burman will give to an officer—that he is clever, painstaking, honest, energetic, kind? No; but that he has "auza." And what is "auza"? It is that influence and power that comes from personality. Who has "auza" nowadays? No one, not even Government. It has become, as Eversley expected, a Commission of Schoolmasters.

CHAPTER V

CRIMINAL LAW

Let us turn now from the *personnel* of government to its methods, from its men to its laws, from the motive power to the machine it works, or which more often now works government.

The first subject that comes naturally to our view is the prevention and suppression of crime, for in point of time that precedes all else. When you are conquering a country, after the soldiers have partly done their work and the civil power comes in, its first care is to create and maintain peace. It organises a police and appoints magistrates. Thus in point of time the Criminal Courts are the first to be organised and criminal law to be laid down, and they are the foundation-stone on which all else is built. And they remain always the most important of the functions of government. If they work well, then there is a good beginning made, but if ill, then the outlook is bad. If what should be Courts of Justice cease in the opinion of the people to be so, then is the very foundation-stone of your rule dissolving. The whole edifice is undermined; it is not founded on a rock, but on something that decays, which soon will give way and let down everything.

Let us go back therefore to the beginning, and see how things worked then. The laws were few, were crude, were often bad. It must be remembered that a hundred years ago the penal laws in England were the most savage, the most useless, the most wicked the world has ever seen. The law in India could not therefore be expected to be very good. But previous to our rule there was no law at all generally. And these bad laws of ours came to the people through the medium of personalities who were for the most part intelligent and sympathetic. Moreover, there was nothing like the number of cases then as now. The system now obliges all cognisable crime to be reported even if petty in its nature. In those days very little crime was reported, it was dealt with by the village communities and never known to the Courts. There were few pleaders; and a trial was really what it ought to be, an inquiry into facts by a magistrate desiring to know them. The question of personality came in a great deal, and whatever may be alleged of the ordinary district courts of those days, they were human, they really tried to be Courts of Justice, they tried to understand. The people respected them. If they did not respect the law, at all events they respected the magistrate who tried to do his best with it. They had an admiration for his personality which went a long way.

Now that is all changed.

The law has been greatly improved. It has been codified by trained legists;

Lord Macaulay and Sir James Stephen were two of them, and it is up to the standard of European codes. But, on the other hand, it has been made absolute. There is a reign of law now, and there is no person in the world who does not hate law when he sees it. The personality that softened it in the old days has been ruled out. The High Courts supervise all work and reduce it to a dead level of uniformity. There is even a fixed scale of punishment sometimes. On revision, cases are rejudged on the written evidence alone. Of course, the case cannot be altered on revision, but the magistrate can be admonished—and he is. All humanity is eliminated.

Therefore the Courts are despised and hated by the people, who misuse them in every way they can.

Let us look into this matter.

In the first place, let me explode a common fallacy. It is frequently said that Oriental people do not dislike crime, that they condone it, that they have low standards in matters of current morality. Therefore they are not anxious to have crime brought to justice as we are. They are a bad lot, and the criminal being but a trifle worse than the average they sympathise with him.

All that is wicked nonsense. Standards in the East are the same as they are elsewhere. The people dislike crime as much as we do. But they think our laws and Courts are not calculated to reduce crime, and they have good reason for so thinking. Moreover, they distinguish between the sinner and his sin—we don't. There lies the difference. Let us consider, therefore, the Courts and their relation to the people.

I confine myself to the province of Burma which I know best, but there is little difference between it and other provinces in these matters. The law is uniform, the procedure uniform, and what differences exist are due to interference of the High Courts acting within the law. In the Indian Penal Code are laid down definitions of the various offences; what it is that constitutes theft, or robbery, or murder. It was drawn out by skilled and able men from the experience of all civilised nations. It is not, of course, perfect; no code could be that or near it, but it is good. With most of it the people have no quarrel. A theft is the same anywhere, and so is a murder. With one point, however, they profoundly disagree, and that is the classification of offences. Theft, no matter how trivial, is an offence against the State, is not compoundable, and is cognisable by the police; whereas an assault, no matter how severe, unless it causes grievous hurt, is the opposite. It is a purely private matter, with which the police have no business. If the sufferer wants to prosecute he must do so himself; pay his own expenses and engage his own pleader, or go without. This is a difference that offends his own instinct. Just take two cases.

Your servant steals a little silver ornament, a few rupees you left about; or some hungry loafer takes some fruit off your tree. You may not forgive him, you may not overlook it. You are bound by law to tell the police and get the offender arrested and convicted. By the petty theft public morality has been outraged, and you must assist morality to vindicate itself. You have no option. If you do not tell the police, you are "compounding a felony," and may be punished. Having told the police you will have no further trouble. They will get up the case, look up evidence, summon the witnesses, prosecute the case, and you will be paid for giving evidence. The thief will be sent to gaol. But if your enemy meets you in the fields, knocks you down, rolls you in the dust, dishonours and abases you in your own esteem and before all who know of it, public morality is not offended. It is of no use going to the police-station; they will not listen to you, they will not prosecute, nor take any notice. If you desire justice you must go yourself to Court, pay to have a petition written, pay for a stamp, get an advocate and pay him, pay for summonses to witnesses, spend, say, three or four pounds, and eventually your enemy may be fined five shillings, of which you, if lucky, may get two as compensation. You may, if you like, at any time withdraw your complaint, if, for instance, your enemy apologises to you or compensates you. Now these are not selected cases, exaggerated cases, nor unusual cases. They are common, and in both cases the instincts of the people are outraged. They are not sordid-minded. A petty theft is not to them a very serious thing. They put a higher value on their personal dignity and self-respect than on a trifling piece of property. To them, therefore, all this is wrong. Theft is never a very deadly offence, and if of small things is easily forgiven. *But they may not forgive*. If the police hear of it, they must give evidence against the culprit—or must lie. They lie. Who blames them? The concealment of thefts, the refusal to report them to the police, the subsequent refusal to give evidence, are common. Is theirs the fault? On the other hand, as it is impossible in the Courts to get any satisfaction for an assault, the hot-tempered Burman seeks revenge in other ways. The Court fails him, so he takes the law into his own hands. He will waylay, will stab, will sometimes murder. Then Government grieves over the large number of serious-hurt cases and wonders what causes them. The wily Madrassi or Bengali coolie gets square in a different way. The injured complainant goes off straight to the police-station and there describes the assault more or less correctly. This, of course, he knows will not help him, so he adds as follows: "During the assault a rupee dropped out of my pocket, and when A had finished battering me he picked up the rupee and went off with it." This makes the offence "theft," which is cognisable by the police, who go off and arrest B and lock him up. Of course, at the trial the experienced magistrate detects the truth, firmly disbelieves the rupee, and convicts A of an assault only. But B is quite satisfied. Has not A been locked up for a week?

The perspective therefore of the Indian Penal Code is wrong. It is taken from English law, which is also wrong, that is, opposed to common sense. How it arose I know, but this is not the place to enter into that.

Therefore the very definition and classification of offences are repugnant to the people, and are themselves causes of evasion: the Indian Penal Code itself is wrong. But that is nothing to the wrong-headedness of the Criminal Procedure Code.

For whereas the Penal Code only partly offends the people, the Court procedure is wrong from top to bottom. Its very foundation principle is wrong.

What is its principle of a trial? Is it a means of finding out the truth? Is it an impartial inquiry into what has happened? Not in the least. A trial is a duel. It is the lineal descendant of the duels of the Middle Ages. The place is changed, it is a Court and not a field; weapons are witnesses and tongues, not swords nor spears; the parties fight by champions, not in person, and the umpire is called a judge, but the principle is the same. Take any criminal trial. On one side is the Crown prosecutor, on the other the advocate of the accused. They fight. All through the case they fight. The prosecutor calls his witnesses, asks them only the questions the answers to which will help his case. The other champion cross-examines, bullies, confuses them, tries to make them contradict themselves, drags in irrelevant matter, and tries to destroy what the other side has built. When the defence is on, the state of affairs is reversed. Neither wants the truth, and only the truth, and all the truth. Each plays to win, and that alone. If either knows evidence which would help the other side he suppresses it. The judge is almost helpless. He has to take what is given. He sees *lacunae* in the evidence, he cannot fill them. He can't get down from off the bench and go out into the country finding evidence for himself. He knows that every witness brought before him has been tutored—not directly perhaps, but indirectly by suggestion, by question, by influence. The case is cooked before it reaches him, and therefore hopeless. He knows he never finds out the exact truth about any single thing. How should he? He knows and sees that witnesses are lying. He knows the reason, because it is a duel, and they are, on one side or another, fighting for vengeance, fighting for liberty. He knows that though they are a singularly truthful people outside, yet inside, their consciences absolve them from the necessity of truth because the Court is so constituted as not to be a place for an inquiry into truth, but the arena of a duel.

He sees cases bought and sold. A clever barrister or advocate will secure an acquittal where a cheaper man would fail. That is notorious everywhere. Otherwise how do great barristers come by their big fees? Clients do not pay for nothing. A barrister is worthy of his hire. The poor man loses and the rich man wins. The poor man goes to gaol, the rich is acquitted or gets a light sentence. So it happens everywhere. The exact truth of a case is never known. For twenty years I was a magistrate and judge. I tried hundreds of cases and I did my best with each. But I never once reached my own standard of understanding. What is that standard? Not that of Courts of Appeal who generally upheld my cases. My standard was this: Do I know enough of the case to write a story embodying it if I wanted to? I never did. For the standard of truth that goes to even the slightest story is very far beyond what is required or possible in even the most carefully heard case.

Now this is not an edifying state of things. It is not edifying anywhere, and I have often heard remarks about it in England from men who happened into a court of law to hear a case. To judges, lawyers, and barristers this view of the proceedings does not occur, because they have been brought up to it, and therefore their minds are locked as far as really appreciating it goes. In India and Burma it is even less edifying. I have often heard Burmans talk of it. "Here on one side are the police, trained men, with all the power and resource of a great Government behind them, trying to get a conviction. They have gone about the country, searched out evidence, tested it, summoned it, and displayed it to its best effect in Court. On the other side is a poor devil of a villager who has been locked up while the police were free; who is poor, who is ignorant, who if he can afford a pleader at all can only afford a very indifferent one. His case is not presented at all, or is very badly presented. True, the case has to be clearly proved or he is acquitted, but the same facts may wear very different colours, according to whether the whole truth is known or only a half. The magistrate does his best, but he can only act on the evidence. The police want a conviction because otherwise their records are bad and promotion is stopped. Do you wonder that sympathy is often with the accused?"

So I have often been asked; and I don't wonder. I often felt that way myself.

When a man first falls into an offence his immediate instinct is to confess to somebody. That is true of all the world. In Burma at the beginning he used to confess to the Court. He was sorry for his offence, he wanted to make the best of it, wanted help to reform. He wanted understanding. He thought the Court wanted to know the truth and he would do all he could to help. But he very soon found the uselessness of this. He got no understanding, no sympathy, only conviction and a vindictive punishment. Naturally he reflected, and pleaders and people who knew the Courts helped him to reflect.

"Fight it out. At worst you can but lose and be no worse off than if you confessed. Why tell the truth? *No one expects you to*. If you have confessed withdraw your confession. Say you were tortured. A trial is a fight, with the judge as umpire. Do your best. Remember that, even if your offence be a very small one, if it is a cognisable offence you will be ruined for life if convicted." That is the advice he gets. Who will doubt but that, our Courts being what they are, it is sound as a rule? So, because it is a fight he won't confess; he plays for the big stake—acquittal; and sometimes this acts disastrously too. I will tell a case in point—one I tried myself.

A man was accused of maiming a bullock. It had trespassed into his Indian-corn field, and had been found there afterwards hamstrung, and had to be destroyed. It was proved that accused was in the field when the bullock wandered in. It was also proved that accused's chopper was found close to the maimed bullock, covered with blood. Accused had run away and had only been arrested some days later.

Now the malicious maiming of a valuable bullock is a serious offence. Its seriousness partly depends on the value of the animal. The case was quite clearly proved though no one actually saw the offence committed. The defence of the accused was a futile *alibi*. He had a pleader who arranged this. The evidence for the prosecution seemed quite clear, and I did not see how I could avoid convicting the man of the grave offence. Yet somehow I was not quite happy in my mind. I believed the prosecution was substantially true, but that they had been piling it on a good deal. So before adjourning the case till next day to give me time to write the judgment, I said to the accused:

"I don't believe your *alibi*. You can see for yourself it has no sense. But maybe if you told me your side of the story it might not look so bad for you as it does now."

He looked at me, hesitated, looked at his pleader, then all of a sudden he did bring the whole story out.

And as he told it, though it did not in any way invalidate the evidence for the prosecution, it did put the matter in quite a new light.

In the first place, the cattle, of which the bullock was one, had been wilfully driven into his field to annoy him and cause him loss. In the second place, he had not deliberately cut the bullock; when he saw the cattle coming through the six-foot-high corn towards him he had in a passion thrown his chopper at the dimly seen moving mass of cattle. Then he had dodged out of their way. When he found afterwards what damage he had done he ran away in a fright.

I found there was evidence to support what he said—for instance, he had gone straight home and told his father before he ran away—so he got off with a small fine. He might have got two years. But unless he had confessed I could never have guessed that there was quite another version of the facts.

Now I have often suspected this state of affairs. The substance of the prosecution is clear, but there might be extenuating circumstances. The accused however fights it to the last and will admit nothing. On the evidence I could but take a gloomy view; for, remember, all cases are subject to revision by the High Court, who simply read through the written evidence and are not able to appreciate the subtle effect of tone and manner in witnesses, which tell more sometimes than their words.

I have said that the people have no respect for the Courts because they have lost all respect for the magistrate or judge. In himself he may be worthy of all confidence; but when on the bench he is not himself, he is a mouthpiece of the law, or an umpire; he is not a living force. When you lie in Court you do not deceive a human being who is doing his best for you and others; you only try to counterbalance the injustice of the law by a little judicious weighting of the scales. A man who will tell you the truth as individual to individual will commit perjury before you in Courts and think nothing of it. In fact, he lies at the other side, and doesn't consider you at all. He does it to try to get justice, or what he thinks is justice, in place of law, which otherwise is all he would get. I have often been told this, and I notice the same in England. Truth is a relationship of persons; in a Court now the only persons are the two opponents; the judge is only a sort of machine to weigh evidence. As man to man I have found Orientals as truthful as Englishmen. In twenty-six years' experience I do not remember ever having been told a deliberate lie as man to man. But in the Courts you are not a man, you are an official, and even as an official your hands are tied. The parties have no direct relationship with you. Their relationship is with each other—just as in a duel or a prize-fight the relationship is between party and party, and the umpire is only the onlooker, who may or may not see most of the game. In law he usually sees less because Justice is blind. I am aware that the bandage over the eyes of Justice is supposed to render her just, not discriminating between rich and poor; it does the reverse, of course. And until Justice opens her eyes again to discriminate what is put into her scales she will remain the mock she now is.

In a previous book I have discussed the question of veracity in this connection, and lest anyone should object that what I say is true only of the Burmese I will add this story, which is of a well-known official in the North-West in his younger days.

He was inquiring into a Revenue case, and incidentally an Indian gentleman gave him certain information. The official thought this so important that he summoned the Indian to Court, where, much to the Englishman's surprise, the Indian as a witness gave a totally different story.

They met again, however, later, and the official asked the Indian gentleman what he meant by going back on his words like that. The latter smiled, hesitated, and then the wisdom of experience spoke to the altruism of ignorance in these words: "Sahib," he said, "you are very young."

How the Courts are generally regarded by the people can best be illustrated by giving an account of a dramatic entertainment I witnessed once. The Burmese are fond of the drama. They have old dramas, and they have new dramas up to date—satires for the most part. The play I saw was of the latter. The company was a well-known one, which had toured almost all the province, and its most famous piece was that I witnessed—I forget the name.

The scene was supposed to be the office of a lawyer, barrister, or advocate, and there was a native clerk. To him entered a would-be litigant. The clerk listens to him for a few minutes and then asks him if he has brought any money. The client says "No." The clerk rises in indignation and the client is hustled out.

He returns with a bag of money. The clerk then listens and the client explains his case. The clerk demands if there is any evidence. The client is puzzled and asks what evidence is required. The clerk then tells him slowly and distinctly: you must have a man to swear to this, another to swear to that, a third to swear to something else.

The client remonstrates, saying he doubts if he can get so much evidence. The clerk then tells him that if he cannot get the evidence demanded his master will not take up his case. "But," says the client indignantly, "it is a true case." "What does that matter?" asks the clerk cynically. "No Court cares—or can tell if it did care—whether your case is true or not. It can only tell if you have evidence or not. If you can't get the evidence your case may be the truest in the world, but that won't help you."

The client then wants his money back, but the clerk clings to the bag and the client is again thrown out. The play was a long one, and I can only give a résumé of parts of it. The client goes looking for witnesses in the village. He gets hold of one man and says: "Come and give evidence." "But I saw nothing," says the villager. "And," says the client indignantly, "would you let me, an old friend, lose what you know is a right cause just because you didn't happen to see a trifle like that? What does it matter if you didn't actually see it? It did happen. I am not asking you to tell a lie or invent anything."

So he gets his witnesses and takes them to the clerk. The clerk takes down their statements. The last scene is in Court, and the client's advocate appears to plead for him. He does so with a tongue two feet in length. But still he loses his case, for the advocate on the other side has a tongue three feet long. That this play was the success it proved to be shows clearly that the audience saw nothing unnatural in it. In fact, they relished it immensely.

The magistrate was a stuffed figure.

CHAPTER VI

PENAL LAW (PROCEDURE)

There is a further difference in their view of crime, between Englishmen as they are made by education and Orientals who in some ways remain the natural man, which greatly affects the Courts, that is the punishment due for crime.

In England we have had the most cruel penal laws ever known. It is not a hundred years ago that there were two hundred and twenty-three different offences for which the capital punishment was awarded. I wonder if people nowadays ever realise their horrors. I have an account of how a poor little servant girl convicted of having stolen some few clothes was dragged out half-dead with fear to a gibbet without the village and there slowly done to death before a crowd of people. It was no unusual thing, for theft of over five shillings was punishable with death. The record of our Courts in England is the most brutal and most bloody in history. They have been reformed but very partially. There is still amongst Englishmen a vindictiveness towards the criminal that is unknown elsewhere. Despite frequent denunciation of the uselessness and the wickedness of vindictive punishment, the idea continually recurs. It is not merely excused—it is even counted as righteousness by those who maintain it.

Now it would be impossible here to give a full analysis of the cause of this vindictiveness. It has many causes. It is not natural, but caused by education. But a principal one lies in our theology. A theology that predicates a God who devotes poor mortals He made to torture by fire for ever, simply for the fun of watching them suffer, has elevated cruelty, uselessness, and vindictiveness into a divine attribute. Therefore men may be excused and even praised for imitating their God as far as in them lies.

The East is free from any such theology. I am not an admirer of any of the theories at the base of its religions, but, at all events, none of them have sunk to such a depth as this. Therefore the Oriental thought is free in this matter to discern the truth.

And further, even the ordinary villagers are deeper psychologists than we are. How this comes about I am not sure; by the free life of the children I think mainly. But however it comes there is no doubt of the fact, for it has been widely noticed. They are very quick at gauging character, in weighing virtues and defects, at seeing in effects the causes. Thus, all throughout the East the fatality that runs through life has been seen; it has even passed into a saying. By fatality, of course, is not meant that God fore-ordains all events, but that every act has its antecedent, that it never stands alone but is the outcome of the past. There has been endless discussion in Europe on this question, but to the East the matter presents itself in very simple guise. No man has the choice of when he is born, into what sort of a physique, of what parents or country. Neither has he any control over how he is brought up, whether educated or not. Thus he himself is to a very great extent a creature not of his own will but of what we may call Fate. He has, moreover, no control over his environment; he did not make the laws, the customs, nor the religion, which surround him. Many of his acts are done under the authority of others—parents, teachers, masters, government; others are the inevitable result of the environment (which he did not make) acting on his personality (which he did not make). There is also chance—as we call it; sudden temptation for instance. Therefore his ability to exercise freewill in act is small, and to hold him personally responsible for all his acts is absurd. Especially is this the case with crime. No one originally wants to commit crime; if he fall into it, his "will" is not usually to blame. A famine will cause a great deal of crime; the criminals did not make the famine. An unusual strain was put on them, and they were not able to stand the strain. Everyone is a potential criminal—given the circumstances. It is more than probable that everyone has at one time or another committed some offence. This is well known in the East, for they think there a great deal more than is supposed. They have not been educated not to think yet. I have myself discussed this point with many Orientals, and I have found that this clear view of the causation of crime is not unusual. Even if the matter has not been thought out there is an instinctive differentiation between a criminal and his crime. They, as I have said before, hate crime, but that shrinking from the criminal so common with us is not so marked with them.

Thus they have long ago seen the futility of attributing crime to a defect of the individual will; they know it is due to much deeper, wider causes. They have also seen the very narrow limits within which punishment avails. Therefore our punishments shock them by their cruelty. Ordinary cattle are worth from twenty to fifty shillings a head, and they roam about the forest on the outskirts of the fields almost unguarded. Yet the theft of one is punishable always with two years' rigorous imprisonment; that is to say, the man is vindictively and uselessly punished, is turned into a confirmed criminal and ruined for life for failing at a momentary temptation. I have known cases where a man was sentenced to ten years' penal servitude for stealing a few rupees—a piece of savagery that the Court sought to justify by the fact that the man had committed several previous petty thefts. Of course, the reason of his repeated crime was the man's inability to earn a livelihood and exercise self-control. He should have been taught and helped—not sent to penal servitude. So are the instincts of the people outraged.

I wonder how many people there are in this world who have not committed some criminal offence; few I should think, and those not the most useful of mankind. I have just been reading of Mark Twain's boyhood, and how, besides "borrowing" many articles, he and his friend "hooked" a boat, painted it red so that the owner should not recognise it, and kept it.

For that in England a hundred years ago he could and probably would have been hanged if caught. In Burma to-day he *might*, after conviction, be let off under the first offender sections, but he would most probably be sent to a reformatory. Yet who thinks the worse of Mark Twain for it?

We think we have reformed our laws and made them common-sense, but we have not. They are still wicked beyond computation.

In *The Soul of a People*, and in I think every book since, I have animadverted upon the uselessness and cruelty of our penal system. When a man has committed a crime, what do we do? Find out the weakness which led to it and cure that weakness—turn him out a whole and healthy man again? No. We make him worse. We make a confirmed criminal of him. Is that sense, to say nothing of humanity? A man who has committed a theft is not past cure; a man who has been in gaol generally is. The people see this clearly enough—that in helping to get a man convicted they are not improving matters for themselves. The offender will come out of gaol a more dangerous character to his village than when he went in. For they go back to their village; they are not thrown loose in a great city as in England. If in England an offender on his release had to be accepted back into his community, the uselessness of our penal system would soon come home to the public. But we have no communities now in England, only an amorphous herd of voters.

All this, however, is clear enough to the East. Therefore they often won't report their losses. They would sooner submit to the small monetary loss than have it on their consciences that they have ruined a man for life. And all for what? Not even to rescue what they have lost, for the bullock is usually dead and eaten, and no compensation is ever given.

The quantity of reported crime in Burma is bad enough, but what would it be if all crimes were reported? Double, I should think. I have known innumerable cases in my own experience where no report was made even of serious offences for this reason. One was a case of attempted murder.

Thus there is a great and dangerous gap between the people and the Courts, and there is no way of bridging it. In England also there is that gap, but it is not so wide, and there are juries who can partly bridge it. In Burma, practically speaking, for Burmans trial by jury does not exist. There is nothing between the accused and the rigid injustice of the laws. The judge and the magistrate are helpless; they must follow the law or be pulled up by the High Court. But a jury need not give its reasons; its future does not depend on the Appellate Court; it is independent, and therein lies its strength and its usefulness. It is juries that put common sense into laws and Courts.

Here is a case in point where Europeans were concerned. There was a certain big firm, and one day it discovered that it had lost certain sums of money—not very large. It could not find out how the loss had occurred; the partners inquired in secret, but could find no evidence. However, they suspected their cashier. They knew he was hard up; they heard he had been gambling. But they had no proof. What did they do? Amend their system of accounts and supervision to prevent loss in the future? No. They laid a trap. They put a large sum within their cashier's reach in such a way that it would seem he could take it—at any rate for a short time—with safety. He took it, and they prosecuted him. The case, I think, was clear, but to the astonishment of the judge, the jury acquitted the cashier. They gave no reasons, of course, in Court. They simply said "Not guilty," and there was an end; but once out of Court they were not so silent.

"Why did we acquit? Because the firm laid a trap. They deliberately tempted him, knowing him to be hard up. He was not charged with taking the first small sums, and in our belief he never took them. Probably he took the last big sum. But why? Because they tempted him. The firm were accessory, they were abettors of the crime. Of course we acquitted."

And I think the general common sense of the community was with them. No one has a right to tempt to crime and prosecute if the crime occurs. But had accused been a Burman he would have got seven years without a doubt. The Englishman got justice, a Burman would have got only law. The Burmans are not blind, do not suppose it; they see this difference well enough.

Nothing could demonstrate more conclusively how utterly out of touch with the people the Courts are, how useless in preventing crime, than the fact that every year Government in despair prosecutes, and either holds to heavy security, or sends to gaol with hard labour for from six months to two years (mainly two years), over two thousand persons who are not only not convicted of any offence, but *are not accused of any offence*. The exact number in 1910 was 2143.

This is done under the Preventive sections of the Criminal Procedure Code, and anything more unjust, more useless, more provocative of crime than this misuse of the sections it is impossible to imagine. The legitimate use of these preventive sections is simple enough. They are to meet the case of the police hearing that a crime, say a robbery, is being planned, and that to prevent its occurring, the would-be criminals may be called on by a magistrate to find security to be of good behaviour.

But such cases are rare and the sections are misused. There are general circulars in force obliging magistrates and police to use these sections to their utmost. When officers are on tour they are enjoined to demand at each village they visit if there are any idle or doubtful characters about, and if so, to prosecute them. Pressure is brought to bear on headmen to produce such characters, and they do produce—everyone they have reason to dislike.

The evidence is all hearsay. Here is a summary:

Question by Police: Do you know Accused?

Answer by Headman: Yes.

Q. What sort of character has he?

Ans. A bad character.

Q. What sort of bad character?

Ans. Well, when B.'s headcloth was missing last year, Accused was supposed to have taken it.

Q. You therefore consider him a thief?

Ans. Yes.

Three such witnesses, and if Accused cannot find substantial security, away he goes to hard labour for two years. This has gone on for the last twenty years. In 1910 one judge has actually opened his eyes wide enough to see that it is a way of manufacturing criminals, and the High Court go so far as to have "misgivings." But there it ends.

There are in Burma now probably 60,000 or more men who have been deliberately made into criminals by Government. No wonder crime is bad.

What is to be done?

The Indian people have clamoured for trial by jury of their peers—that is their fellow-countrymen—but it has always been refused. Government does not say why—but the reason is well known—it is because it fears that juries would invariably acquit. And that fear is probably justified. Judging from what assessors do I should say it was fully justified. They would acquit. But does not this very fact indicate that the law and the people are at variance? It most emphatically does not mean that the Orientals condone crime; it means that they think that crime is now wrongly dealt with. There was a period in England when juries would not convict. Why? Because they condoned crime? No, but because the punishments were too brutal; and the law had to be altered till their consciences were satisfied. That was the way the old penal laws came to be amended. When juries won't convict it is because their consciences are being outraged in some way. Has any attempt ever been made to discover in what way our Courts in India now outrage the people's consciences? Never to my knowledge. There has been the fixed idea that our system is perfect, therefore blame the people. "They must have Oriental minds which no one can understand."

The Indian Penal Code is the principal law relating to offences and punishments, but there are many minor laws and all are defective in the same way—that they have been framed out of some inner consciousness, and not out of practical knowledge.

Take the Gambling Acts in Burma. The Burmese are a cheerful people, and, like other cheerful human beings, they like their game of chance sometimes. When it becomes a public nuisance, of course it must be checked, no one doubts that; but the Gambling Acts go much farther than that. The people have not a great variety of games, and their principal card game is a sort of bank. It can, of course, become a big gamble, but it can also be as innocent as penny loo. Nevertheless, it is always illegal because there is a banker. That is the way the Act is framed. So if five or six villagers gather in the evening for a game at penny loo they can be raided, tried, and fined or imprisoned. I had a Burmese subordinate magistrate once who was not only a very "energetic" officer but a very religious officer, and he determined to stop all this "pernicious gambling" in his township. He established a "terror," so to speak. He had censors everywhere, and if a schoolboy tossed another double or quits for a farthing, the law was after them.

I could not stop him because he had the law behind him, but every month I sent for all his gambling cases on revision, and I quashed them all. There wasn't any Appellate Court behind me in those matters and I had a free hand. Finally, as he wouldn't take a hint, I got my too energetic assistant transferred to other fields of usefulness.

It doesn't look well for Englishmen to play bridge and other games of cards for money in their Clubs and bungalows while the Burmese are totally debarred. It smacks of self-righteousness. A good deal of our rule does that now, and it does not tend to make it popular. In human affairs there are a time and a place for things, but in law there is only the absolute. Now the absolute is wrong. And if there is one quality above another that is detestable it is self-righteousness. Our laws tend to self-righteousness; our judges and officials are very liable to succumb to that tendency. It is bad for a man to have to deal continually with the seamy side of human nature; he can only keep his mind sweet by continual touch with the other side. But in India and Burma the ordinary official knows nothing of the other side. He has no dealing with the people except in an official capacity. He knows nothing of their ordinary life, their work, or their amusements. He does not take an interest in the staple industries of his villages, nor in the amusements of the people. Therefore he cannot see how bad the laws are because he judges them *a priori* and not in relation to their effects on the people. The Indian Penal Code he knows, the accused and the witnesses he does not know; the Village Act he knows, the village organism he is hopelessly ignorant of. Therefore when Government pass and enforce laws that do more harm than good he cannot tell them what is wrong. Naturally, he must believe nothing is wrong.

Yet the whole Penal System of India is wrong. It is very wrong indeed. I believe I could keep a district in greater quietness and peace if its Criminal Courts were abolished altogether and I were allowed to use the village organism in its proper form for preventing crime. For the essential truth in dealing with crime, as with disease, is that it can be prevented but can rarely be cured. However, I do not mean to say that Criminal Courts, if they administered good laws and were reasonably constituted, are bad things. They will in time be to crime what hospitals are to diseases: places where the sufferer goes to have his illness diagnosed and cured so that he come out a clean man whom the community will be glad to welcome back. That a man who has once been in gaol is for ever a social leper is the strongest condemnation a system of criminal justice could receive.

As things are now the people hate the Courts; they hate the law, all of it. It must not be supposed that, because I have pointed out only certain defects, all the rest is satisfactory. That is very far from being the case. But my object is not to criticise the laws or Courts exhaustively. I only want to dissipate the complacency that regards them as perfect and the people alone to be blameworthy. There is no one who more dislikes pointing out deficiencies than I do. If I could I would never write anything but pleasant things. But that is impossible. An imminent danger hangs over our Indian Empire, and so our own future and its can only be secured by facing the truth. If Indian officials on the spot would open their eyes and see things as they are there would be no cause to write—but they will not.

CHAPTER VII

THE CIVIL COURTS (CIVIL LAW)

We come now to the Civil Courts, wherein all suits relating to property, to inheritance, and to money are tried.

I have already referred to the archaic state in which, all over India, matters of marriage and inheritance remain; no change has taken place during our rule, nor could do so. Except in Burma, all these matters are connected with religion, and although people when in a progressive state will themselves not hesitate to break through fetters of religion and custom, they will never allow a foreign Government to do so. Our Government interferes already in a great many matters it had better leave alone, and to lay a sacrilegious finger on domestic concerns would cause instant antagonism. It is not our business. Is Government thus to intrude into the very home? You can imagine the howl there would be, and rightly. We must not touch them, and the people, disorganised as they are, cannot touch them; so there they remain.

In a previous book I have referred to the Burmese law that no one may make a will, and to its effect in preventing Burmans building up a business. Moreover, the law of inheritance is so doubtful sometimes that when a rich Burman dies his estate usually goes into Court and, naturally, does not come out again. This is very unsatisfactory, but until there is some real self-government I see no help for it. On a matter of this kind it is of no use collecting the opinions of any number of Burmans as to what should be done, and so passing an Act. It is a fact to which I shall have to revert later that men as individuals will give an opinion, which if combined into an assembly with authority to act they would greatly modify. Moreover, if our Government were responsible, individuals would urge action, which if they themselves were responsible they would not take. No advice that is not steadied by a sense of responsibility is of much value. Our Government cannot deal with such matters. Only a body representing Burmese opinion and responsible to that opinion could do it. There is not now any prospect of any such body. The present Councils are useless. There may be such a body in course of time, but until there is, matters must remain as they are. The result is discontent, naturally.

Take another similar point. In Upper Burma a good deal of the land is what is called ancestral land; that is to say, in private hands. Now there was amongst the people a great pride in holding land their ancestors held, and such land is very rarely sold. I am not quite sure that it can be sold. Neither is it mortgaged in the usual sense. What the owner does is to hand the land over to a mortgagee for a sum of money. He pays no interest on the debt because the mortgagee enjoys the land. Such a transaction is called a usufructuary mortgage. The owner can at any time redeem the land by repaying the original loan. In Burmese time there was no period of limitation, but our Limitation Act has imposed a limit of sixty years. Thus a man may hand over a piece of land to a mortgagee, go off to Lower Burma—as many have—and at any time within sixty years he or his heirs can redeem the land for the same sum.

Consider what this means. I am the mortgagee of a piece of land. If I improve it so that its value is increased the owner can come back, borrow money to redeem it, and re-mortgage it for double the amount next day to someone else. Therefore I certainly won't improve it. I can't sell it. I can work it of course. I have also to defend my title every now and then from attack. It may be that the original mortgagor did not own the land at all. He may have simply been the member of the family in whom the occupation was vested. The other members can challenge my right. They do. And this sort of thing can go on for sixty years. That is not the sort of law to encourage progress. It encourages litigation, but that is all. The whole country groans under it naturally. But before any relief could be given there would have to be some consensus of opinion among the people as to the change. Government could not do it themselves. Even if their amendment were good it would raise a hornets' nest about their ears.

Thus here again is an *impasse,* and a dangerous one, typical of many.

By our system of Civil Law and Civil Courts, of precedent and case law we have petrified the bonds in which India lay when we arrived and made them far more rigid than before. While by our introduction of new ideas and of greater material progress we have rendered the old laws more and more obsolete, we have at the same time stopped all evolution of these laws, and killed any capacity they had for accommodating themselves to change. Some lawyers even, enthusiastic as they are about their own profession, have seen this danger. Here is what Sir Henry Sumner Maine, who was Legal Member to the Government of India, says:

"What that law and usage"—Indian law and usage—"was, the Sudder Court used to ascertain with what some would call most conscientious accuracy and others the most technical narrowness. Under the hand of the Judges of the Sudder Courts the native rules hardened and contracted a rigidity which they never had in real native practice. Among the older records of their proceedings may be found injunctions couched in the technical language of English Chancery proceedings which forbid the priests of a particular temple to injure a rival fane by painting the face of their idol red instead of yellow, and decrees allowing the complaint of other priests that they were injured in property and repute because their neighbours rang a bell at a particular moment of their services. There is in truth but little doubt that until education began to cause the natives of India to absorb Western ideas for themselves the influence of the English rather retarded than hastened the mental development of the race."

And it does so more and more, because however much they may absorb Western ideas theoretically, they cannot express them practically owing to our petrifaction of their law and custom.

Again. "The methods of interpretation which the Sudder Courts borrowed from the Supreme Courts imported from Westminster Hall put a stop to any natural growth and improvement of Hindu law."

That is to say we introduced new ideas, but sat on the safety-valve lest they should produce any effect. Sir Henry Sumner Maine's book is full of similar expressions, but I need quote no more. Those who wish to read how a lawyer himself has admitted this failure of law will no doubt read the book for themselves.

And now let us go on to the other functions of the Civil Courts—money decrees and so forth.

I do not think that they are any more in touch with the public than the Criminal Courts.

To begin with, they suffer from the same defect that a trial before a Civil Court is not an inquiry into truth, but a duel between parties. Indeed this is even more manifest than in the Criminal Courts, for there the magistrate does to the best of his small ability go outside the record and try to ascertain facts for himself; in the Civil Courts the judge never does so. He is simply and purely an umpire. Has the plaintiff proved his case? If so, give him a decree; if not, then not. Therefore perjury, and even forgery, are more common here than in the Criminal Courts.

Now let us go back to the way suits originate, and see what the cause is.

There are, of course, a few cases where the issue is clear from the first. A dies. B and C both claim his inheritance. Here from the beginning is a clear issue which can be brought into Court and fought out. It must come into Court, because in no other way could it be settled. But there are few such suits. In the great majority of cases the original issue is quite a small one, but when it comes into Court it is, by one side or the other, or both, swollen out of all recognition. Take the following as an example. It is from a case I heard once.

A and B were both natives of India—Hindus—and had been partners. I cannot remember their business beyond that they bought articles in Upper India and imported them into Upper Burma, where they sold them. It was a small business. One partner would go to India, buy stock, and return with it to Burma. They would both trade in it, and when it was nearly done one of them would go away to India again. This had gone on for some years. They agreed together excellently and made a decent profit. They kept all their accounts in their heads, aided by an occasional scrap of memoranda, and made a settlement from time to time.

Then they would begin afresh.

At last came a disagreement.

When A returned to Burma with a new stock, B objected to the price paid for one item, alleging that A had been "done," and had paid too much.

A indignantly repelled this accusation. B stood to his guns. The item was only about five hundred rupees, and the difference was not more than twenty or thirty rupees, but neither would give way.

The quarrel grew. B said he would not share in the item; A said he must, as it was a partnership transaction. B said he didn't care. A said he would sue him in Court. B said, "Very well, sue me." So each went off to get a pleader.

In due time the case came into Court, but what a case! Each side had considered that if he had got to fight he had better get all the weapons he could, so he raked up everything he could think of. It was a duel, you see, wherein each side fought not to settle the little point at issue, but for victory—any kind of victory he could get. Each side stirred up every sleeping dog of war he could find, resuscitated and galvanised dead dogs, made up imitation dogs, and came to battle.

The issues finally framed covered several years' transactions, and the evidence included forged documents and quantities of perjury. Both sides were ruined.

That is what comes of making a trial a duel. Each side fights for victory, to save his *amour propre*, and to wound the enemy wherever he can. The original cause of difference is quite lost.

Now that case is typical of many. It is illustrative of human nature all the world over. If you awake the fighting instinct you cannot confine the parties to the original seat of war; they will urge the attack wherever they are likely to win. They cannot go to the judge in the beginning as to a friend of both parties who will inquire into the cause of difference himself and find a reasonable settlement, because judges are not intended to do that. Therefore parties do not go to Court at all until they have determined to fight it out. The case does not come to Court till matters are hopeless.

You may say they should or could have gone to an arbitrator. Do people anywhere in the world trust an unofficial arbitrator? There is a provision in Upper Burma allowing reference to arbitration, but it is a dead letter.

The original dispute in this case was about twenty or thirty rupees, the alleged excess paid for the goods. The suit filed was for several thousand rupees in transactions spread over years: there was an equally heavy counterclaim.

The total value of the suits filed in Burma in 1910 was about £1,380,000. I wonder what the value was of the matters first in dispute before the cases came to Court. A fifth, I dare say, would cover them. I notice much the same thing in England. Human nature does not differ East or West.

Now consider the enormous expense of all this. The value of the subject-matter of suits filed in Burma in 1910 was, as I have said, £1,380,000. The value of the matters really in dispute before they came to Court was infinitely less, but Court fees and lawyers' fees had to be paid on the full amount. Witnesses in thousands were called to prove matters that should never have come into Court at all.

And with what result?

There were 70,203 suits filed and decrees given, but in 53,594 of these satisfaction could not be obtained, and so the decree-holders had to come to Court for warrants for execution. That is to say that in over five suits out of seven the losing party could not or would not pay. (It does not follow that in the other two out of the seven he did pay. The decree-holder in a percentage of cases no doubt did not think it worth while to go any further.)

But in 53,594 cases he came to Court for execution. What did he get? In half these cases he got absolutely nothing; the execution was "wholly infructuous." In the other cases satisfaction was obtained in full or in part.

Thus out of £1,380,000 claimed how much was obtained? The Report does not give figures, but the reader can judge for himself it wasn't much. And to get even this little, what was the cost to the litigants, that is the public? No one knows. But there are a great many lawyers of kinds in Burma, and a good deal of money goes into their hands.

I do not think it would be an over-estimate to say that for every pound originally in dispute two pounds were spent in costs and only ten shillings recovered, and to get this, think of the trouble, the worry, the indignity, and the self-contempt involved. Besides, think of the waste of time—to say nothing of truth.

In the Report from which I take these figures the Judges of the High Court point out that the Courts are yearly becoming less and less used by the public. They can't think how this can be; but they suppose it is due to years of prosperity. That it should be due to anything wrong about the Courts never occurs to them. Yet perhaps the reader will see reason to doubt if the system of Civil Justice is perfect.

There is an Indian proverb that it is wise to go to law once, foolish to go twice. I asked an Indian about this.

"Why is it wise to go once?" I asked.

"Because," he answered, "you learn a great deal, quite a great deal, which you never forget. You learn, anyhow, not to go twice."

"But," I objected, "suppose on a subsequent occasion money were due to you which you couldn't get, would you sit down under the loss?"

He looked at me and laughed. "Well," he said, "if it were a small debt I should let it go. If I thought the man could not pay I would let it go, big or little; but if I thought he could pay and wouldn't, I wouldn't sue him; no, but I wouldn't put up with him either."

"What then would you do?"

"Well," he answered reflectively, "I think I should rob him."

"But that might bring you into a Criminal Court," I remonstrated.

"So it might," he replied; "but the Criminal Courts can't be worse than the Civil; and, anyhow, it would be a change."

As to the Insolvent side of the Civil Courts, perhaps if I say that it is no nearer the people than any other side, enough will have been said, and later on I shall have a story to tell of some of my experiences, but this is not the place.

What is gained by imprisoning a man for debt? Nothing that I ever heard of. It is not required to deter him from being ruined again; he probably won't get the chance, and if he did the fact of having been sold up once is quite sufficient deterrent from wanting to be sold up again.

Will it deter others? People don't get ruined for the fun of the thing. It is a dreadful thing to be sold up; in itself that is quite enough. Then what good does imprisoning the poor devil do? It does none. It does harm, and nothing but harm. It hurts the debtor and prevents his recovering himself; it panders to the desire of society and of creditors for revenge. There is an idea abroad that when anything untoward happens somebody should be punished, and then society will have vindicated itself. But the duty of society is to prevent crime, not punish it, and it cannot whitewash itself in this way. It merely condemns itself more even than it condemns him it punishes.

Moreover, the ability of creditors to imprison debtors is misused in a way that is almost criminal. The creditor will imprison the debtor with the hope that the debtor's relatives and friends will subscribe to save him and them from this disgrace. That is to say, the law allows a creditor to put improper pressure on totally innocent people in order to get his claims satisfied. Think of the iniquity of a law like that!

And what are these claims? Are they just claims? They are legal claims, but are they just?

For the most part they are claims of money-lenders. The Courts act as collecting agencies to the most oppressive system of money-lending that can be imagined. Two and a half per-cent per month is not unusual.

Government has shown its recognition of this danger by creating Co-operative Credit Banks, which are a great boon. But it has not thought of revising its Civil Court procedure. As in most other matters, it recognises something wrong, but attributes it to the people, not to the Courts and the law; therefore it does nothing.

But at all events imprisonment for debt should be abolished. There were eight hundred unfortunate debtors imprisoned in Burma in 1910.

Do you wonder that the people dread and hate the Courts?

Civil law embraces a great variety of suits besides suits for money, and includes a great number of special laws. The harm that has been done by fossilising Hindu, Mohammedan, and Buddhist law and custom has been already mentioned; to enter further into these matters is unnecessary. Once it is clearly recognised that the law and the Courts require amendment, not in details but in fundamental principles, there will be many better critics than I am. For although I have been obliged to learn some law in order to do my work, I was never an apt student of it. Humanity and justice are the only studies I really care for. Law is mainly a denial of both. Therefore if the Government of India and the local officials will but give up thinking that where law and human nature disagree it is so much the worse for human nature, they will soon find out where the present laws are wrong. But before I close this chapter there is one further point I wish to mention, and that is the trial of Burmese divorce suits by our Courts. Now that is wrong, absolutely wrong, and indefensible in every way. The Courts are not concerned with divorce. It is by Burmese custom and common sense a purely village matter. Divorces can be given by the elders, and they alone should be allowed to pronounce them. For they are sensible men, and in such cases they act not as judges, but as neighbours. They will grant no divorce till they have exhausted all means of conciliation. They know the parties as no judge can know them; they know who is to blame, how he or she is to blame, how the difference can be adjusted. It is to their interest to smooth things down and prevent their getting worse. Theoretically the breakers of marriages, they are in fact the preservers of marriage. It is by their tact and common sense that couples are kept together, and that only when matters become impossible divorces are granted.

But a judge is different. He knows nothing, cares nothing, can do nothing but listen to the complaint and grant the divorce. It must legally be granted at the request of either party, remember. To allow a judge to try divorce cases is a violation of Burmese law and custom, and is another and deep injury to the village community. How and why it was ever allowed I don't know. I suppose no one ever thought about it. Divorces in England are granted by Courts according to English law, therefore in Burma divorces can be granted according to Burmese law. I suppose that was the argument—if ever there was any argument at all.

In any case it is wrong. Divorces are properly granted by the elders acting on behalf of the community, and by no one else. Therefore the interference of the Courts should be immediately stopped.

But apart from this, the questions of marriage and inheritance are very difficult. No alien Government can solve them. They must await a real Council that can deal with such matters with knowledge and responsibility.

CHAPTER VIII
THE VILLAGE

But of all the errors of Indian government, none is so serious as their destruction of the Village organism throughout India; none has had such an effect in the past; none is likely to have such bad consequences in the future.

It is the Village policy of government that has created for it the most difficulties, and which is at the bottom of the most serious unrest. For it touches not merely a few as criminal law, but practically all the population; it affects not only a part of the life of India, but it has injured it in its most vital point. In the whole history of administration there is nothing I think so demonstrative of the ignorance of government as the Village policy.

The foundation on which not only all government but all civilisation rests throughout the world is the village. As this is contrary to the usual idea that civilisation rests on the family it will be convenient to shortly show how this is so. The village is the microcosm of the State, because it includes within it divers trades and occupations and races and religions and castes in one community. A family does not do so. A family is by its nature of one blood, it is almost always of one occupation. There are families of cultivators, merchants, priests, lawyers, smiths, and so on. It is of one religion, of one caste, of one habit of thought. A family is narrow and a village is broad. Families divide; villages combine. Societies organised on the family, or clan, or tribe principle have always failed—by the very nature of things they must so fail. The Jews are a race, or tribe, and not a nation. They have no civilisation of their own, but adopt that in which they live. The Highland clans had to be broken before the Highlands could be civilised. The caste system in India ruined its old civilisation, and is the bar to any new civilisation. The Turkish Empire is dead because it was based on a religious caste divided from all others by a mutilation, and its people could never amalgamate with others. There is a continual flow of peoples to and fro upon the earth, and village communities absorb the new-comers and thereby acquire new blood, and, what is far more important, new ideas, to add to the old and leaven them. Families, classes and tribes cannot do this. They become stereotyped, and dissolve or die. Thus the basis of all civilisation has been the village, or in later times the town. The decay and death of all civilisations have been preceded by the death of the local unit. Thus imperial Rome was itself doomed to death when it destroyed local life; and a new civilisation could not be built up till the local communities had attained a fresh life. Florence, Genoa, Milan, Pisa, Venice, and many others made the civilisation of the Renaissance. So in England, a free Parliament was made up of representatives from free cities and counties. These have been destroyed, and the present constituencies are merely so many voters. Policies are no longer decided in Parliament, but in secret party conclave. Members are the nominees of that conclave, not of free local organisms, and Parliament has become a machine to register its decrees. So are free institutions passing away.

There is no lesson of history more true—more certain—than this, that the village or town is the unit of all free life and civilisation. It contains all classes, different races, religions, castes and forms of thought, and is therefore a real unit.

Now these units have existed all over the world, and when civilisations and governments have disappeared they have been built up anew from the villages. In India the village system was the one organism that survived the long years of anarchy and invasion, and it was in full vigour when we conquered India. Those who care to read up the subject can see it in Sir Henry Sumner Maine's *Indian Village Communities*.

In Upper Burma, on its annexation in 1885, the village community was strong and healthy; it alone survived the fall of King Thibaw's Government. Then we deliberately destroyed it, as we had destroyed it before all through India.

Now this is an instructive and interesting fact, for it was destroyed in ignorance, not by *malice prepense*.

Throughout India—and especially in Burma—you will find Government reiterating its conviction of the importance of preserving the village organism, repeating the conviction of its absolute necessity, and at the same time killing it. This is but an instance of much of the action of Government. It means well; it does actually see the end to be attained—it has no idea how to attain that end; but, instead, it renders it impossible.

If I explain what happened in Burma, the history, *mutatis mutandis*, of what has occurred throughout India will be clear.

In the first place, a "village" does not mean only one collection of houses; it is a territorial unit of from one to a hundred square miles. Originally, of course, there was in each unit one hamlet; but, as population grew, daughter hamlets were thrown off. They still, however, remained under the jurisdiction of the mother hamlet, and they all together formed one village. In each village there were a Headman and a Council of Elders. The headman was appointed or rather approved by the Burmese Government for life or good behaviour; the council was not recognised by law. Notwithstanding this, the council was the real power. It was not formally elected, it had no legal standing, but it was the real power. The headman was only its representative and not its master; he was but *primus inter pares*.

This headman and council ruled all village matters. They settled the house sites, the rights of way, the marriage of boys and girls, divorces, public manners; they put up such public works as were done, they divided the tax amongst the inhabitants according to their means, and were collectively responsible for the whole. There was hardly any appeal from their decision, but the power not being localised in an individual but in a council of all the elders, things went well. The village was a real living organism, within which people learned to act together, to bear and forbear; there were a local patriotism and a local pride. Within it lay the germ of unlimited progress.

The English Government on taking over Upper Burma recognised the extreme value of this organisation. In Lower Burma much of our difficulty arose from the fact that the organisation was wanting and that between Government and the individual there was no one. So one of the first efforts of Government in Upper Burma was to endeavour to preserve and strengthen this local self-government. Unfortunately every effort it made resulted in destroying it rather than consolidating it. A wrong view was taken from the beginning.

The council was ignored. How this happened I do not know, I can only suppose that it arose from ignorance. The only man recognised by the Burmese Government we replaced was the headman. They dealt directly with him and not with the council. They did not appoint the council or regulate it in any way. In law no council existed. Therefore, when we took over, the law was mistaken for the fact—a common mistake, due to seeking for knowledge in papers, and not in life—and the council was ignored. The following seems to have been the argument: Government appointed the headman, therefore he was an official. Government did not appoint or recognise any council, therefore there was no council. Anyhow, that was the decision arrived at and enforced.

There is on record a circular of the Local Government in which the headman of a village is described as a Government official; to be to his village what the District Officer is to his district. That is disastrous. A headman is not an official of the Government. His whole value and meaning is that he is a representative of the people before Government. He expresses the collective views of the village and receives the orders of Government for them as a whole. He is *their* head, not a finger of Government. He corresponded almost exactly to the mayor of an English town, who would be insulted if you called him a Government official. Yet this mistaken view was taken of the village headman, and this error has vitiated all dealings of Government with the village organisation and its headman. He is appointed by Government instead of being appointed by the people and approved by Government. He is responsible to Government, not to his village—as he ought to be—for the use or abuse of his powers. He is punished by Government for laxity. By the Village Regulation he can be fined by the District Officer.

There has grown up among Europeans in the East a custom of imposing fines. They fine their servants for breakages and innumerable other small matters, and then complain how scarce good servants are. The clerks in Government offices used to be subject to continual fines until Lord Curzon stopped it. Now headmen of villages can be fined by the District Officer; and they are fined; the proviso is no dead letter. It is a mark of the "energetic" officer to use it. Can there be anything more destructive? Imagine the headman, the mayor of a community of three or four thousand people, fined five shillings for the delay of a return, or set, like a schoolboy, to learn a code—with the clerks. I have seen this done often. What respect for Government, what from his own people, what self-respect, can he retain after such treatment?

Again, by ignoring the council and making the headman an official, Government set up a number of petty tyrants in the villages, free from all control but its own; consequently it has been forced to allow great latitude of appeal. This still further destroys his authority. He is under old custom, legalised by the Village Regulation, empowered to punish his villagers who disobey him in certain matters. The punishments are, of course, trivial. When approved by the council, as in old days, they were final; but now they can be appealed against—and are. A headman who endeavours to enforce his authority runs the risk of being complained against and forced to attend Headquarters, to waste days of valuable time and considerable sums of money to defend himself for having fined a villager a shilling for not mending his fence. One or two experiences of this sort and the headman lets things slide in future.

Thus interference with the village is constant and disastrous. Headmen are bullied, fined, set to learn lessons like children, all in the name of efficiency. And Government wonders why the village system decays. A continual complaint of Government is that headmen are no longer the men they used to be, that they have lost authority. The best men will not take the appointment—and who can wonder? Here is a story in illustration:

There was a small village in my district, on a main road, and the headman died. It was necessary to appoint a new one. But no one would take the appointment. The elders were asked to nominate a man, but no one would take the nomination. I sent the Township Officer to try to arrange; he failed.

Now a village cannot get along without a headman. Government is at an end; no taxes can be collected, for instance; therefore it was necessary a headman be appointed at once. I went to the village myself and called the elders and gave them an order that they must nominate someone. So next morning, after stormy meetings in the village, a man was brought to me and introduced as the headman-elect. He was dirty, ill-clad, and not at all the sort of man I should have cared to appoint, nor one whom it would be supposed the villagers would care to accept. Yet he was the only nominee.

"What is your occupation?" I asked.

He said he had none.

"What tax did you pay last year?" I asked him this in order to discover his standing, for men are rated according to their means.

He told me that he had paid five shillings—less than a third of the average.

"You are willing to be headman?" I asked.

"No," he said frankly. "But no one would take the place, and the elders told me I must. They said they would prosecute me under the 'bad livelihood' section if I didn't. I could take my choice between being headman or a term in prison."

This was, of course, an extreme case, but it illustrates the position. The headman is degraded and all administration suffers.

It is the same in municipalities. The work is done by the District Officer because it is easier for him to do it than to instruct and allow others to do it.

The people one and all hate this. The headman hates it, because though he is given much greater power nominally than he used to have he dare not use this power. He is isolated from his villagers, and so often becomes an object of dislike to them. Through him orders are enforced which are not liked by the people, and he has to bear all the brunt. His dignity is gone. Sometimes he is murdered.

The elders hate it. They have been ignored. They are placed under a headman who may or may not attend to what they say. They have lost all interest—because all power—in their village affairs. They have no responsibility.

The villagers hate it. A council of their own elders they could respect and submit to; a one-man rule they detest. Their appeal to the council on the spot (who know) has been lost; and in place of it they have an appeal to a distant officer who, with the best will in the world, cannot know. An appeal costs money, and even to win may be to lose. They all want to manage their affairs; they can do it far better than we can, and there is nothing they so much appreciate as being allowed to do so. Here is how I learnt this:

Some eighteen years ago I was leaving a station where I had been for a year as subordinate officer, and had to cross the river by launch to the steamer station on the other shore. I went down to the bank to get the launch, but it was late. I saw it three miles away, and so sat down under a tree to wait.

Presently two or three elderly Burmans came and sat down near me. Then came others, till maybe twenty elderly men were there. I recognised two or three vaguely, but none clearly. I wondered at their being there, and asked:

"Are you crossing over too?"

They shook their heads.

"What are you here for, then?"

They looked embarrassed, and at last one spoke. "We came to say 'Good-bye' to you."

I stared. "But I do not know you, except that I suppose you are elders of the town."

"We are," they said, "and you do not know us because you have not ever worried us in any way. When we had business together you did it quickly and decisively; otherwise you left us alone. You did not treat us as children. Therefore we are sorry you are going."

I laughed. I could not help it. To come and express regret at a man's leaving on the ground that they knew next to nothing of him and did not want to know more seemed unusual.

But it was true. And often, after, did I think over that "send-off" and take the lesson to heart.

Now what is true in Burma is true over all India. The local circumstances of course vary. A lumbadar in the North-West, for instance, does not quite correspond to a headman in Burma. The actual form in which the village was organised differs from place to place according to local needs. Even in Burma it differed a good deal. But the differences were only of form. In all India there were self-contained village communities within which, to a certain extent, caste, religion, and race were subordinated to local communal feeling.

And everywhere Government has killed it by turning the village officials into Government officials, responsible to Government and not to the village.

Thus there is now absolutely no organism a man can belong to. There are three hundred and fifty million individuals in India, and that is all. They are divided laterally into strata by caste and religion, and there is no influence to draw them together. All organised life is dead. Government by means of its official—the headman—interferes with almost every detail of life, regulating his conduct by rules drawn up in Secretariats by men who never knew what a village was, and the appeal is to another alien officer.

Further, all morality and all conduct are the outcome of corporate life, that is to say, of the village or of a larger unit. Morality is, in fact, where it is useful and true, the knowledge of how to get along with your fellow men and women, what conduct offends them and leads to the injury of society, what pleases them and tends to harmony and mutual happiness. It is not fixed, but adapts itself to changing circumstances of the society, and it is enforced by the opinion of that society.

But injure the society and both manners and morals are shaken. It is a common complaint of India to-day that the bonds of morality have greatly slackened and that manners have almost disappeared. This is attributed to the waning influence of religions. But, generally speaking, religions have not waned in India—on the contrary, their influences have increased. The people have become more and more in the power of religious systems. Therefore the cause given is absurd and untrue. It does not exist. Further, neither morality nor manners are the outcome of religion. On the contrary. Religions claim them to be so, but the claim is false. Manners and morals may be said to be the gravity which binds individuals into a community. They make the community and are themselves the outcome of the community. Destroy the community and you have destroyed the source from which manners and morals arise.

That has been done all through India. In another book I have pointed out how disastrously this has acted in Burma and how much the people feel it. I do not want to repeat myself. But if those officials who deplore the frequent cases of young girls running away with boys, of seduction, of adultery and other offences, of immature marriages, and other mistakes, would but realise that all these arise from the injury we have caused to society, there might be a change. All the human virtues, with no exception, either arise from or are increased by the aggregation of men into communities, and it is very difficult to keep them alive where no organic communities exist. Consider the words humanity, civilisation, patriotism, urbanity—their derivations and their meanings—and you will see this.

I do not think I need say more. I have tried to set out the facts as clearly and dispassionately as I can. I have omitted much that I might have said. I have tried here, as throughout, to understate difficulties rather than exaggerate them, because exaggeration defeats its own ends. But I think if the reader will try to realise to himself the state of affairs where no village has a say even in its simplest affairs, and where everything is under the eye of a Government official, where all initiative is forbidden and where the best men stand aloof from all interest in village affairs, he will have some idea that unrest is not unreasonable.

The village organism was the one vital institution left to India; it was the one germ of corporate life that could have been encouraged into a larger growth. It has been killed. It will have to be resuscitated before India can cease to be *India Irredenta*.

CHAPTER IX

OPIUM AND EXCISE

I will begin what I have to say about this by telling a little story about what happened to me when I was a Subordinate Magistrate—some sixteen years ago now.

A Burman was brought up before me charged with possessing opium. A Sergeant of Police had met him at a rest-house in the jungle the day before, and had entered into conversation. The man was sickly and told the Sergeant that he was on his way down from the Shan States, where he had gone to trade. But he had caught the prevalent fever, had then lain ill and lost his money. So he was going home again to his village about fifty miles away, where he hoped to recover his health. Meanwhile he took a little opium for the fever, for in the Shan States opium is not contraband.

"Oh, you have opium?" asked the Sergeant.

"I brought some down with me," the man said, producing it. Then the Sergeant, as in duty bound, arrested him and brought him into Court.

The case was quite clear. The man admitted the opium, urged that he was ill, also that he did not know—neither of which is a defence in law—and I passed the smallest sentence that I thought the High Court would allow to pass without a reprimand. I fined him ten rupees or in default ten days' imprisonment. Then I went on to other cases and forgot about it. At four o'clock I left the bench and went to my private room to sign papers before leaving Court. There was a pile of them. I signed, the peon pulled away; I signed again, he pulled; and so on till I looked up. There in the doorway stood the Sergeant. He seemed embarrassed. He smiled an awkward smile, saluted, and then stood doubtfully on one foot and the other.

"Well?" I asked, surprised. "What is the matter?"

"Nothing," he replied.

"Then you needn't stay," I said suggestively, and went on signing. He didn't go. He smiled again and swallowed. I signed a dozen sheets or more and then looked up, and there he was, still smiling.

"Well," I asked, "what is the matter? Out with it."

"We are all poor men," he said.

"Who are?" I asked carelessly.

"All we police," he said. "I gave a whole rupee, but the others could give but a penny or twopence each because they are only constables. We could not afford more. We are poor men, your Honour."

I stopped my signing. "Sergeant," I said, "come here. I don't know what you're talking about. What is the matter?"

"There is a little girl," he answered, coming up to the table. "That's the difficulty."

I held my head between my hands. I had no idea of what he could be talking about. The syncopated method of beginning a conversation which Burmese often use made my head ache. I stared, he stared. At last I said:

"Sergeant, I'm going home," and rose. Then it all came out.

It was the opium smuggler. He could not pay the fine, for he was penniless. He had no friends this side of fifty miles away, and he had with him a little daughter aged ten years or so. This was, of course, the first that I had heard of her, but it seems that she was just outside when her father was being tried, and when she heard he had to go to gaol she was in despair. They wept together.

Therefore the Sergeant whose zeal had caused the trouble repented of his work and took up a collection. In the police-office and among my clerks he got five rupees. That was but half, and they did not know where to get the rest. Then someone had a brilliant idea. "Go," he said to the Sergeant, "ask the magistrate." "Therefore," said the Sergeant, "I came in to your Honour."

"For what?"

"The other five rupees."

I laughed. How could I help it? The audacity of the demand, that I, the magistrate, should pay half the fine that I had myself inflicted!

"Sergeant," I said severely, "what have you and I to do with offenders who break the law? Are we to pay for them? What is the good of *your* arresting them and my fining them if we afterwards pay their fines for them? We make a mockery of the law and ruin ourselves."

He did not answer.

"You see the point?" I asked.

He did.

"Then I am going home."

The Sergeant saluted. "I didn't suppose your Honour has the money in Court. Shall I come for it or will your Honour send it over?" he replied.

"Send what?"

"The five rupees."

I sent it over.

This story, besides illustrating the kindheartedness of the people and their quickness to see the injustice of a law and try to remedy it, shows the difficulty

Government have in this matter of opium.

Now I do not intend to go into this very controversial subject. I have read the evidence and the Report of the Opium Commission some years ago, and I have my own opinion about both. That I will keep to myself. All I have to say here is that opium in reasonable doses is a most valuable drug—the most valuable we have. It is in fever-haunted districts the best friend of the people. Some of the best fighting men of the Empire take it and demand it. In its time and place it is no more harmful than liquor, and I have no belief in putting the world into an iron case of everlasting "Don'ts." People should be made temperate by training and judicious restriction of opportunity, and not made the slaves of laws. I don't believe in slavery of any kind.

But opium can be and is abused, and there is no doubt that amongst the Burmese generally there is a desire that its use be totally prohibited. A general opinion like that should be respected whether it is right or wrong.

There comes the difficulty. Take Burma as a whole and consider it. The vast majority of the inhabitants are Burmese, but in places in Lower Burma there are large colonies of Hindus and Mohammedans. There are, moreover, many Chinese traders and carpenters spread about all over. They are accustomed to use opium, were so accustomed before they came there, would not have come if they could not have got their stimulant.

Then, again, Burma is bounded on the east by the independent Shan States, where there is a great deal of fever, where opium grows, and the people use it. Beyond these States is China, where opium is grown largely. Moreover, there are in Lower Burma one or two districts where fever is very deadly and opium is used by the Burmans with the consent of public opinion.

Now sum up all these factors, and see how complicated the problem is.

The Burmans generally want opium prohibited. "Very well," says Government; "we will prohibit it for Burmans; but what about the rest of the population? They want it; their public opinion does not forbid it. They are immigrants, and would not have come if they had been unable to get it. Therefore there must be opium shops for them. But Burmans shall not be allowed to buy."

So far so good in appearance. The Burman may not buy from the shop, and doesn't. He buys from a friendly Chinaman, who for a little commission buys the opium at the shop and hands it over outside.

But this trick was discovered, and Government did its best. It allowanced all Chinamen. They could buy so much and no more, just enough for their own use. If they sold to Burmans they had to go without themselves.

That was excellent, only there were two ways round. One was for Chinamen who did not use opium—not all do—to act as honest broker; the other was smuggling from the Shan States. The quantity of opium smuggled down from the Shan States cannot be estimated, nor can it be stopped. How can you guard five hundred miles of frontier all mountain and forest, intersected by forest paths? Opium is light, compact, easily concealed. Government does its best, but it cannot do the impossible.

Therefore the Acts are widely evaded, which is always a bad thing; but there is a worse effect than this—there is discrimination by nationality.

I do not think there can be anything worse than an Act that says such and such an act is right and proper for people of one nationality but wrong and penal for people of another. A Chinaman may walk about and do openly what if a Burman does he goes to gaol for. What difference is there between the natures of the two people to make such a difference? There is none. Therefore the effect of this law, although it be according to the general desire, is to make the Burman feel that he is a child not to be trusted. This is a bad feeling. If opium were totally prohibited in Upper Burma for everybody except Indian troops or officials sent there by Government, and therefore not free to stay away, this feeling would not arise. If local option is to have effect it should be by areas and not races.

The same thing applies to alcohol. An Indian coolie can go and buy some liquor and have a drink with his friends. A Burman may not. At least not of licit liquor. Therefore a great deal of illicit liquor is distilled.

Try to see how demoralising all this is. Take a town like Sagaing, my last head-quarters, which is really only a big village, and note the results. There is a liquor shop where European liquors, beer, and spirits are sold, and there are several shops where native spirits are sold. A European, or half-caste, or Hindu, or Mohammedan of the better classes could go and buy a bottle of Bass or of Dyer's ale at the European shop and take it home for dinner. The Burmese magistrates, inspectors of police, and so on could not—legally. My Treasury officer, being a Burman, was debarred; his subordinate, a native of India, was not debarred. What happens? Well, I don't know. But I bought a pony once from a very respectable and able Burmese Inspector of Police, and the first morning I rode him he took me gently but firmly to the back door of the liquor shop. That gave me an idea, but I kept the idea to myself. I have often had ideas of this nature.

Then take the poorer classes. Is it good for one race of people to see another making merry with a glass while it is illegal for them to do so? Does it not create bitterness, to say the least? Does it not perpetuate differences that must disappear if self-government is to succeed?

Here, again, if laws are to succeed they must be in accordance with the desires of the people. Only the people at large can stop smuggling. Read the history of how English smuggling was stopped; it was because no one could smuggle without being informed on—that is to say, public opinion had turned against them.

But that is not so in Burma. Were prohibition of opium or spirits by localities where all were treated alike, you could ask the people to help you to enforce their wish. But for opium and liquor to be sold to some and refused to others is not a local option. No one likes it, and no one will help to stop smuggling. That is human nature.

Government has been and is greatly abused for its opium and liquor policy, but I think if facts are looked at squarely it will be

> seen that the situation is very difficult. The only way out that I can see is through local self-government. If the scheme that I sketch out at the end of this book took form there would be local option eventually, and people will submit to what they themselves enact, whereas they chafe against the same thing when imposed from above. That is human nature, and it is a very valuable trait of human nature. It is the revolt against subjection, and the declaration that the objective of life is to be free. The only morality of any value comes from within; that imposed from without may improve the body, but it enervates the soul. Now the body is temporary and the soul eternal.

Here I may end my criticism of the machinery of government. Not that any of the other branches of the administration are better than those I have written of. The land laws are, I think, worse, because they are based on imported fixed ideas and not on any careful investigation of facts and the underlying causes of facts. The police administration is bad; the village administration worse than bad. But I do not want to criticise; I want to establish my point, which is that the unrest in India is a legitimate unrest, that it is not factitious or political, but based on very real grievances that must grow till they are relieved.

I have picked out these four branches of the administration: the Criminal and Civil Courts, the Villages, and the Opium and Excise, for specific reasons. The reason I chose the first two is because no one ever seems to have suspected before how bad they were. Everyone has gone on the fixed idea that because the magistrates and judges are honest and the law up to date there can be nothing to complain of in them. The fault must be in the people.

Only as I write I get a letter to this effect from an officer of long experience. He had "never seen anything wrong with the Courts." Therefore I have set out the facts to the best of my ability. I want the reader to see for himself. I don't want him to accept my authority that they are bad; I don't believe in authority. I want him to think over the facts I have laid before him and frame his own judgment. I think that he will see that the Courts which have been declared impregnable are very vulnerable indeed.

The reason I chose the Village is because it is the unit of self-government.

The reason I chose the Opium and Excise was different. Whereas Government has never been criticised for its Courts and its law, which are bad, it has received unending criticism for its Opium and Excise policy. Yet, mistakes apart, I don't see how it is much to blame. The difficulties are inherent. They are the same in nature as those that beset liquor legislation in England. The question has not been solved here; far from it. In fact, it is insoluble by Act; it is only soluble by education of the individual. The right and temperate use of alcohol and drugs is a personal, not a State question. Therefore where Government could have been criticised it was not, and where it did its best in great difficulties it was abused. This will give a key to another difficulty in India: Government receives hardly any good and useful criticism from any side. It is abused and praised, but that understanding criticism which is of the greatest value to individuals and Governments is wanting. The Indians are feeling serious unrest, and they cannot diagnose the cause—no one can diagnose himself—so they strike out at random against Government measures and officials. They are like a certain party in England who also are unhappy with things as they are, and who express their dissatisfaction at, say, the marriage laws—which were made not by man, but by Churches, whose great supporters were and are women—by smashing the orchid house at Kew. It reminds me of Andrew Lang's ghost. What he wanted to say was that the drains were out of order and a danger to all the inhabitants of the castle. But he suffered from aphasia, and the nearest he could get to an indication of his meaning was driving round and round the castle at midnight in a hearse and four.

Most changes arising in societies are incoherent in the same way, but it must not be supposed that because the expression is irrelevant there is no real and serious cause beneath it. When an overboiling kettle spills and scalds the cat who never did the kettle any harm, it is hard luck on the cat, but it is not unnatural in the kettle. And it would be dangerous therefore to stop up the spout. Later on the kettle might explode and damage the cat's master.

The English papers in India want to support Government, which is right; but the best support they could give would be to point out where Government goes wrong and help it to go right. They never do that, because the editors live in towns and know nothing of the country. Moreover, they too suffer from fixed ideas.

It is the same with the criticism the Indian Government gets from England. There are here practically only two parties. One says, "Sit tight on the safety-valve and shoot anyone who comes near you"; and the other says "Give government to the people." Now there is no organised Indian people as yet to give it to.

No Government has ever had so little help from intelligent criticism as the Indian Government; none ever needed it more. No Government in the world is more sincerely desirous of the good of the people it governs; none knows so little how to secure it.

You cannot have any work done efficiently unless there is honest and understanding criticism. No sensible person objects to it if it is given sincerely and fairly. But that is not so in India. Considering how unfair most criticism of the Indian Government is, it shows great self-restraint in the consideration it accords to it. And you can't expect Government officials to criticise themselves. It isn't part of their functions and it isn't fair to ask it. Their duty is to carry out the laws and orders they receive. They have neither the time nor the attitude of mind to be always criticising them.

But there ought to be somebody whose function is to investigate the working of government, and to suggest and criticise. In England it used to be done—badly—by Parliament and the papers. Now no one does it: everyone now only seeks "party" advantage. In China there used to be censors whose duty it was, I am told, to watch the working of the machine and criticise it. That would be an admirable idea if it could be carried out.

The Government of India should have censors. They should be well paid, and

I think their lives would have to be heavily insured. Their reports should not be pigeon-holed, but published.

At present this ill-informed criticism of Government has succeeded in achieving one and is pressing another measure for the alleviation of the unrest which can do nothing but harm. The danger is that Government, not knowing the right thing to do and pressed to do something, will accept these measures rather than be accused of ignoring the unrest.

India is lost to us—lost in spirit, and only awaiting the opportunity to be lost in substance. How shall she be regained?

Government have two ideas. Let us see what these are.

PART II
COUNSELS OF DESPAIR

CHAPTER X

THE PROVINCIAL COUNCILS

The first step that has been taken with the hope of allaying the discontent in India has been the increase in the Councils of the Government of India and of the Local Governments of Madras and Bombay, with the creation of Councils in the other Provinces which did not have them before.

And as these Councils have been in certain quarters greatly praised as being not only good in themselves now but as containing the germs of great possibilities, it is necessary to consider them carefully.

Councils were first instituted in India in 1861, were enlarged in 1892, and again much enlarged in 1909; thus they are no new thing, and their value is already fairly obvious. Moreover, since the enlargements of the Act of 1909 some time has elapsed, so that I am not here criticising institutions which have not yet had a chance of showing what they can do.

There are Executive Councils for the Government of India and for the Provincial Governments of Bombay and Madras, and there are Legislative Councils for the Government of India and for each Province.

The whole of the law for the constitution of these Councils is contained in the Indian Councils Acts of 1861, 1892, and 1909, and the Rules for the nomination or election of the members are contained in Blue Book Number Cd 6714, published in 1913. I give these references in order that anyone who cares to go into the subject in greater detail than I can in this chapter will be able to find all his material readily. He will be able to see how other Councils than those I intend to deal with here are constituted; also in what way and by what constituencies elected members are chosen. There is a great deal that might well be said on each of these Councils.

But the only Councils I propose to deal with here are those of the Government of India and of the Province of Burma. I would have liked to include the Council of Madras but that I think the subject can be fairly understood without this.

The Executive Council of the Government of India consists of the Governor-General and nine members. These form the Cabinet of India, and, subject to the control of the Secretary of State, it has supreme power. It includes the Commander-in-Chief and members for Finance, Public Works, Home affairs and so on.

The only alteration made in this Council is by declaring that one of the members must be an Indian. So far that member has been the Law Member, and it is somewhat difficult to see how any other post could be filled by an Indian. You can find Indian lawyers, many, perhaps too many of them, but where are you to find Indians with that necessary experience that would fit them to be Finance or Home Members or Commander-in-Chief, for instance?

The appointment of this Indian gentleman to be Law Member has not been followed by any striking results. Law in India is petrified, and until the great reform takes place petrified it must remain. It does not seem to matter very much who is head of it. When reform comes it will not be an Indian who could undertake it.

The Legislative Council is formed of the Executive Council and Additional Members. Before 1909, Additional Members were few, they were nominated and there was always a good Government majority. Since 1909 it has been constituted as follows:

Nominated Members
28 officials
5 non-officials.

Of these five non-officials one is to represent the Indian Commercial community, one the Mohammedans of the Punjab, and one the landowners in the Punjab. The other two nominated members may be anyone apparently.

Then there are twenty-seven elected members; two each to represent the four large Provincial Councils; one each for the five smaller Provinces, one each to represent the landowners of six Provinces; five representatives of Mohammedans in these five Provinces; one member each to the Chambers of Commerce of Bengal and Bombay; and one extra Mohammedan member. Thus in this assembly there are represented in a way nine Provinces as wholes, the landowning class of some Provinces, one religion and the trade of two cities.

To make it clearer to the reader who has not been to India, let me put it in this way. India is as big as Europe without Russia, and has three hundred million inhabitants, more than Europe. Suppose Europe were conquered and administered by Martians, and they were to establish a Council. If they did it on similar principles to this Legislative Council of the Government of India it would consist of:

Two members each for Germany, France, Great Britain, and Italy, one member each for five smaller nations, one representative each for the landowners in Great Britain, France, Germany, Italy, Austria, and Spain, five representatives of Protestants as Protestants, and one each for the Chambers of Commerce of London and Paris.

What would the reader think of this as a Council to make laws for all Europe? What would he say? I think he would say many things. He would also ask some questions. He would ask:

Firstly, how can two members represent great countries—like England for instance? Or one represent another great area and people like Spain? Is it conceivably possible that one or at best two individuals could have the necessary knowledge or impartiality to do this?

His second question would be: How can one man represent landowners spread over a great territory with different forms of tenure, different crops, different climates, different nationalities?

His third would be: Two cities are represented; where are the others?

His fourth would be: At best, all these members can but represent, in even ever so faint a way, their own class who elects them. Say at a liberal estimate that they represent more or less imperfectly half a million people; what about the two hundred and ninety-nine and a half million who are left out? Who are to protect tenants from landlords, the innumerable unrepresented religions from that one which is represented, the voiceless cities from the two which have voices? In fact, who is to protect Europe from these few privileged classes?

That would be analogous to what is happening in India. These questions are being asked.

The answer to the first question is quite simple. The two members do not represent Madras, nor does the one member represent Burma. They represent the non-officials of the Local Council, and that is all; that is to say, ten or fifteen individuals of much their own class and standing. It is not likely that they have any knowledge of the country they are to represent, except the chief town. It is quite certain that they have never even travelled over half their country, nor speak more than one or two of the various tongues.

They have no knowledge of the administration anywhere, nor any administrative ability. If a question vital to their Province arose they would not know what to do; and if they did know they would not dare to do it if it involved any responsibility, because they have no backing in the country supposed to be theirs. They are totally unknown, even by name, to nine hundred and ninety-nine out of every thousand inhabitants. In fact, even this is an over-estimate. They are not only without knowledge of the immense majority of "their" people, but are antagonistic in race and religion to many of them, so that it is only the English Government that keeps the peace.

The answer to the second question is much the same as to the first. Fancy one member representing the Nair landholders of Malabar, the Poligars, the Tamils, the Telugu landholders, and many others. It is absurd.

There is no answer to the third question.

The answer to the fourth is that whatever help and representation and defence the bulk of India can obtain must be obtained from the English official members. They alone are quite impartial; they may be comparatively ignorant, but their ignorance is light compared to that of the native members, for it includes a knowledge of administration obtained by experience, which none of the latter have. It is we alone who have raised the people economically, and have done it often enough against the influence of class.

Therefore the Council of the Government of India is so constituted that whereas perhaps half a million people are represented directly or indirectly by class and religion, the two hundred and ninety-nine and a half million have no representation at all and must depend on the English officials.

This is no new discovery of mine. Here is what Lord Curzon said in the debate in the House of Lords on this new Act: "I wonder how these changes will in the last resort affect the great mass of the people of India—the people who have no vote and have scarcely a voice. Remember that to these people, who form the bulk of the population of India, representative government and electoral institutions are nothing whatever. I have a misgiving that this class will not fare much better under these changes than they do now. At any rate, I see no place for them in these enlarged Councils which are to be created, and I am under the strong opinion that as government in India becomes more and more Parliamentary—as will be the inevitable result—so it will become less paternal and less beneficial to the poorer classes of the population." It was seen that these Councils were merely by way of handing over the India we have made to a tiny section of privileged classes whom we were to keep in power and support with our bayonets. It was seen and disregarded. Why?

So much for its constitution. Every principle that experience shows must go to the making of a successful Assembly has been scorned. The representation, even such as it is, is by class, by race, and by religion. No assembly where such a method of representation has been adopted has ever been known. Wherever, even in a small degree, such differences have existed it has paralysed all action. Take, for instance, the French National Assembly before the Revolution. Imagine a House of Commons with members for landowners, for the merchants of London and Glasgow, and special members for the Catholic Irish in England and Scotland. Even that would be far less extraordinary than the Council of India.

This Council has no executive powers, but it can ask questions: it can discuss the Budget though it cannot make alterations; it can make laws affecting all India. But all it does is subject to veto by the Government of India—and naturally so. How could you delegate real power to a Council which, the English officials apart, has no representative value of any kind and no administrative experience? The power behind the Government is the power of England—the Army, the Navy, and the wealth of England. It is administered by British officials, and even the native army is officered by English officers. Is this great English organism to be used for enforcing laws passed by such a Council as that I have described? To be at its mercy, to be its servant? Does it enter into the possibility of things?

The Council, the officials apart, is in reality at its very best advisory only. It cannot be more. It has no power behind it and could be given no responsibility. Yet without the fear of responsibility what advice is ever well given? Irresponsible advisers! Of what value have they ever been in the world's history?

"But"—I have been told and have read often enough—"the Council works well, it is a success, it has gratified the educated Indian. Why criticise it, then?" To that I reply, "In what has its success consisted—what has it done?" And to that I never get any answer except that it is a success because it has done nothing. The speakers were afraid, apparently, it might try to do something—to express, for instance, some of the desires and needs of the people, a few of which I have tried to explain in this book; to suggest some new policy to Government, to show how the great and increasing unrest might be guided into safe channels; and it has been a success because it has done none of these things and was capable of doing none of them. It has been as an influence *nil.* All it has done has been empty criticism. A writer trying to praise it says: "The debates in the Imperial Council are already not unworthy of older and more famous assemblies." If the comparison is with the House of Commons it is not inapt. For many years now debates there have been merely a pretence. The conclusions are already fixed and the speakers know it. They speak to pass time, to satisfy the electors that they are really doing something to justify their existence, and they try to show off—or to score off someone else. Their speeches have no value. They make no difference to the result. And the debates in the India Council are no different. It perhaps gives the members the illusion of power and authority to be able to badger Government and make long speeches, but it can effect nothing. The debates are make-believe. How should they be anything else? The men are not to blame, but the institution.

"But"—again say its advocates—"this is but a beginning. The Council is but in embryo. Wait till it comes to greater maturity."

To what greater maturity can it come? Is there in this Council any true idea that can expand and grow? There is no idea at all. Is it ever contemplated to make it really representative? How many members would it take to represent three hundred millions of people? On the British basis, not a liberal one, it would require an assembly of over four thousand five hundred members. Is that possible?

Is any election possible among the masses of the people?

Is it ever possible that real executive or legislative power should be given to an assembly when it is the English Government and the English people who in the last resort would have to carry out those orders and bear the brunt of their failure?

Think over the facts carefully. Could you make a central Parliament to govern all Europe? No. For a hundred reasons the idea is impossible. It is equally impossible in India. It is even more impossible in India than it would be in Europe.

Finally it is said that this Council has satisfied the educated class in India.

Has it?

And if it had could there be a greater criterion of its worthlessness than such satisfaction?

Let us now turn to the Burma Provincial Council. There is no Executive Council, all executive power lies with the Lieut.-Governor. The Legislative Council consists of seventeen members.

One member is elected by the Chamber of Commerce, and the other sixteen are nominated. Of these sixteen, six may be officials; two experts may be official or non-official; the rest must be non-official; of these, four must be Burmese, one must be Chinese, and one must be Indian.

The Council has power to enact local legislation for Burma only. That is to say it can pass special or local laws. It cannot, of course, interfere with or vary the Imperial legislation, such as the Indian Penal Codes. Its powers are small and are limited. It is, as will be seen, representative of nothing. Except the officials, none of the members have any administrative knowledge; none are known to the people at large even by name. That they approved or passed any Act modifying, say, the Burmese law of inheritance, would be no justification for it before the people. They represent neither people nor ideas. They have effected nothing and can effect nothing because they have no force behind them. What have any of them ever done that the people should repose confidence in them?

For the rest the same criticisms apply as to the Indian Council. The Lieut.-Governor has all the executive power and he has the power of veto over all legislation. Naturally he must have this power. If not, he might be forced into using British power and authority and means for enforcing Acts that he disapproved of and were passed by men who represented at best not one thousandth part of the country.

Yet, as long as he has this power of veto, the Council, like the Indian Council, becomes simply an advisory Council with no responsibility. And, again, of what value is advice that is not steadied by the sense of responsibility?

And with all this talk of self-government, of an Imperial Indian Parliament and local parliaments, of election and representation, there is in no village in the Indian Empire any self-government at all, even in the smallest matters. The villages are one and all under the rule of a Government official, and every vestige of self-government has been destroyed. India may have representatives in the India Council and a voice, even if an impotent voice, in Imperial matters, but it may have no representation in its Village Council, and no voice in the smallest village concern.

The whole base on which any self-government could rest has been destroyed. And instead of building up from below a system of self-government that would proceed from the people and be so founded as to stand any shocks, it is sought to begin self-government from the top, by suspending in the air Councils that rest on nothing, that mean nothing, that have as much solidity and reality as kites would have.

This, too, must have been foreseen, because it is obvious. Why, then, was it done?

Was there ever in any history a *reductio ad absurdum* like these Councils of Despair?

CHAPTER XI

THE INDIAN AS CIVILIAN

The next measure which has insistently been pressed on the Government is that far more Indians should be admitted to the Civil Service. It is now composed almost exclusively of Englishmen, and the conditions are such that it is difficult for Indians to enter. This, it is claimed, should be altered, and the Civil Service should be to a great extent Indianised.

Well, as I have said, the Government of India is not Indian, it is English. It is essentially English, the more so and the more necessarily so because it is in India. It consists of very few members compared to the work it has to do, and it is of the highest importance therefore that it be completely efficient. England has made herself responsible for India, and she cannot shirk or divide this responsibility. She cannot say: "I will by admitting a few Indians into the service shift some of the responsibility onto them and so onto India." That is unthinkable. The Government of India is English, and until by revolution or devolution it disappears it must remain English. It is the Army and Navy of England which ensure India's safety. Therefore her first duty, not only to herself but to India, is to enlist in her superior service such men as will govern most efficiently.

Now to govern efficiently we must govern in our own way. There are not for us nor any people two ways of doing a thing well; there is one way only possible at the time—one way in which the genius of the governing race can best express itself. That is the one we must follow, and to ensure its success we must have in the service men who are not merely by education, but by what is far more important, by instinct, best fitted to carry out the ideas of government. You must have officers who will know what to do not only when they are told, but when they are not told, who, being one in race and feeling with the Government, will instinctively do all in accordance with it.

For it must never be forgotten that the government of India is a very difficult matter, and will always be so. It is not plain-sailing, like the Local Government of any self-governing people, or even of Russia. The administration of India is alien. The system is alien; and though it need not be so much out of touch with the people as it is now, alien it must remain. As long as the government is alien the machinery must be so. Englishmen could not work machinery they did not understand.

Even in self-governed countries there is always a feeling against government. Taxes are hard things to bear. This is shown in socialism and many other ways. But in an alien-governed country like India this discontent is much greater. Government has not only to bear the blame for its own faults, but has to vicariously suffer for the shortcomings of the monsoons and the inroad of plague. It is responsible, in the people's ideas, for everything. The internal peace which is taken for granted in most European countries cannot be so assumed in India. We are very often within measurable distance of riot, and an unchecked riot may quickly develop into an insurrection. The first essential, therefore, of government is the maintenance of peace and the immediate suppression of any symptom of unrest.

Now the forces at the disposal of the authorities are not large. For the whole province of Burma, as large as France and England, and with a thousand miles of wild frontier and ten millions of people, there are only four British and eight Indian regiments. There are, or were, besides (I have not the latest figures) some ten thousand military police, who are men recruited in India and officered by English officers from Indian regiments. The Burmese police are only for civil duty and detection. They are not for "keeping the peace" purposes. For the whole of India there are but 70,000 British troops and 140,000 native for a population of 350,000,000, with a difficult and turbulent frontier. There is manifestly no margin to waste; the resources available must be used with the utmost efficiency. There must be direct understanding and co-operation between the military officers who command the forces and the District Officers who supply the information, the intelligence and the direction. Now if the District Officer were an Indian this could not be. It is no reflection on either the courage or the capacity of the Indian to say this, for the quality necessary is neither of these. It is one which he does not and cannot have, but which is essential for the proper carrying out of his duties. It is *camaraderie* with the other officers.

Official relations between civil and military are always difficult. It is impossible to lay down hard and fast rules defining their respective responsibilities. There is a certain antagonism between the objects each wishes to attain and the way to attain them. The civilian wishes as far as possible to avoid bloodshed; to soothe, not irritate, nor threaten. Fighting is the last thing he wants. The soldier, on the other hand, wants to get at his enemy and have it over; to stir him up if he be not already stirred up enough. He wishes action that is short, sharp, and decisive. The civilian is long-suffering. Therefore disagreements arise, and that these conflicts of official opinion should be minimised, something more is necessary than that the men on both sides be good officers. They must be friends. The rubs of official intercourse must be effaced over the mess-table, the card-table, the camp fire; must be forgotten in talks of home, of mutual friends. How often has it not happened that it has been the mutual appreciation of a poet, the remembrance of a charming woman, the admiration of an opera, that has rendered possible that co-operation which is the soul of work. There must be the continual consciousness on both sides that theirs is not a temporary official relationship. They will meet continually hereafter at other stations, at head-quarters, at dinners, races, clubs—in the East and at home. They must be friends all through; there must be a mutual understanding.

Now if the civilian were an Indian gentleman all this could not occur. That Indians are often honourable and cultured gentlemen I know; that in essence all humanity is one I am never tired of affirming. But there are differences of race, real differences, important differences, differences that the Indian himself should be the last to try to ignore. Every nation is given by nature the qualities peculiar to it and which it is its duty to cultivate for the world's sake. To attempt to sink your individuality in that of another is an injury not only to yourself but to the whole world. An Indian gentleman cannot be an Englishman. It is no use his trying. He only makes himself absurd. He can be something quite as good if he will cultivate his own talent; but he has not our talent. He is not an Englishman, and only an Englishman by birth has that *camaraderie* with other Englishmen that is essential. Even a Frenchman or a German would not have it. Therefore it would be impossible to place Indian civilians in places where co-operation with military or military police-officers would be essential.

Further, it is not the English officers alone who create the difficulty. It is the men—English and native. Men of fighting races in India will not acknowledge the authority of Indians of other nationalities, even if supported by Government.

I will tell a story in illustration.

I was stationed nearly twenty years ago at a district head-quarters in Burma where there was a battalion of Military Police recruited in Upper India. There was also a young Mohammedan civilian who had passed into the Civil Service in London and been posted to Burma. He was an excellent fellow in his way.

It happened one morning that I rode down to the Battalion Commandant's house to see him on some matter. We discussed our business, and after it was finished the Subadar of the battalion, a great soldierly Sikh, came in. He and the Commandant talked for a while, and when he was leaving E. said:

"By the by, Subadar Sahib, we are coming up this evening to the range to do a little firing. Send up the marker and four rifles."

"*Four* rifles?" queried the Subadar.

E. nodded.

"For whom?"

"For the four Sahibs," said E.

The Subadar counted. "The Deputy Sahib, Huzoor (E.), Hall Sahib, and who else?'

"Oh," said he, "Mahommed V. Sahib," naming the Indian civilian.

The Subadar turned away with a gesture of scorn.

"A sahib? he?" he growled.

Now suppose this Indian civilian had grown up into charge of a district and had to direct or go with these men into action? What would happen?

But it may be said that matters could be so arranged that civilians who were Indians were not posted to troublesome or frontier districts, or that they were given judicial and not executive appointments. They make, it is said, good judges. Why keep them out of duties they do well?

But have those who advocate this ever considered what it would mean? It would be the creation of a class within a class. The civilian who was an Indian would be differentiated from the English civilians; he would be ear-marked as "not for executive duties." Is that a possibility, and if it were, would not this differentiation be worse than entirely excluding them? The *corps d'élite* would still remain English and the grievance be where it is.

Let us look facts in the face. The Civil Service of India is a peculiarly English service; it is efficient exactly in so far as it is English; when Indians enter it they must be inefficient more or less. Not only are they not good for the service, but the service is not good for them. They would be better and happier out of it, and they feel that themselves. They have gained their ambition and regret it all their lives. I have known several Indians who were civilians and all were unhappy. One was very much so. This is his story. It all happened a long time ago now, not in Burma, and I do not think any susceptibilities can be hurt by recalling it.

He was a Madrassi of the race and caste of Chettis, not the money-lending Chettis, but another branch who always seek Government service. His people were well off and he was sent to England to school; then to Wren's to study for the Civil Service, into which he passed high up, and after two years at Oxford he came to Madras and was posted to a district on the west coast. He was a nice fellow, clever, agreeable, and most people liked him. In England he had been given access to good society, and no difference had been made between him and his English fellow-students. He expected it would be the same in India. He was a member of the Indian Civil Service and would be accepted as such.

He was not. The first thing that happened was that the Club refused to admit him as a member. Now to the home-staying Englishman this may seem a small matter. It is no essential in England to a man's efficiency, or even to his happiness, that he be member of a social club. It can make no real difference to his career.

In India it is different. The Club in a country station is the centre of everything. Practically every European belongs to it. He does not go occasionally, but every day. At five o'clock, when Courts and offices close, there is a general resort to the Club, for golf, tennis, cards, billiards. Most clubs have a women's wing as well, so that the whole of society is centred in the Club. It is there that matters are arranged and informally discussed. Work is done at Court, but the preliminaries of work are often arranged at the Club; or, if not, the annoyances of work are there removed. You forget over a drink and a cigar what happened between you at Court. Women, too, use their influence at the Club, and women's influence is never negligible. The Club is the real heart of the station's life, and if a man do not belong to it he is outside the organism, so to speak. I am quite sure that no senior officer would do his work if he were outside the Club, and even a junior officer would find it difficult.

Every effort was made to elect Chetty to the Club. The other officials stood by him loyally, but it was no use. The unofficial Englishmen refused to allow an Indian to be a member of the Club. Now it is no use characterising such exclusiveness as wrong, or mischievous, or narrow, and saying it should not exist. It does exist. It always will exist. It is very strong, and it is based on instincts that are good in themselves and cannot be ignored. Club life is only possible to people of one nationality. You cannot mix in a Club. In Rangoon do not the Germans have their own club?

The unofficials threatened if Chetty were proposed to overwhelm him with black-balls, and so his name had to be withdrawn. I may say I do not think his nominal admission as a member would have made much difference. Merely allowing a man to enter a club does not admit him to the intimacy of the Club, and that alone counts. However, Chetty was refused admittance at all.

There were, of course, other troubles. An Indian who has entered the Civil Service is really in an impossible position. Socially he belongs to no world. He has left his own and cannot enter the other. And you cannot divorce social life from official life. They are not two things, but one. In the end Chetty shot himself. It was a sad end for a man gifted and likeable.

And although such an end was unusual, the causes which led to it are universal. I have known several civilians who were Indians, and, as I said before, I think they were all unhappy. They felt that fate had put them in an impossible position. If they married their fellow-country-women they by this act divorced themselves still further from European society; if they married an Englishwoman they did no better; the other Englishwomen would not receive her, and inherent differences of civilisation rendered married life difficult. I think that if individuals realised what their ambition would lead to they would choose any other walk in life than to enter an alien service. Their ideals are wrong. It is no true ideal for an Indian or Burmese to wish to be an Englishman. Fate has allotted to him a different field of usefulness quite as great in its way. An Indian gentleman may be quite as true a gentleman as an English gentleman and be not in the least like him. By blind imitation they attempt to attain virtues not inherent in them, and they ignore other virtues which are inherent and necessary to the world. They seek after impossibilities and so negative the achievement of possibilities. They deny their own natures.

It may be that this desire of Indians to enter the Civil Service has arisen from the desire to begin local self-government—a proper ambition. But the end cannot be attained in this way. Like all other edifices, local self-government is built up from below. It is built on its own foundation. You cannot begin replacing an edifice by removing the top or middle stones and replacing them with others. Self-government is not to be attained by gradually altering the roof.

Therefore the claim that they would influence Government is untenable. Government must do its work in its own way, and that is the English way. No Indian can tell what this is.

The further claim that it would satisfy the people is equally untenable. To put a native of one part of India over natives of another part of India would not please them; it would exasperate them. And even to put an official over his own people would not please those under him, though it might please his class. This is a well-known fact; and if you look below the surface it is not difficult to see the reasons. The Government is English; a native official is not English. The people have no confidence in him for that reason. They know that he is not in intimate touch with

Government. In the innumerable acts of official life which are not bound by rigid rules he is very likely to be wrong. When an English official says a thing they know he speaks with authority because his mind is one with that of Government; not so with a native official. They know it and he knows it, and he knows they know it. That makes matters difficult to begin with. Moreover, they are jealous of him. When all high officials are English, natives are all together; put a native in as an official, and to the general native mind he is rather like a traitor. They have lost him and gained nothing. They are not proud of him but angry with him. He is as they are—why then should he have this power over them? It is not a power delegated by themselves but by an alien Government. This is quite a simple fact in psychology and shows itself everywhere. Does a "ranker," unless under exceptional circumstances and an exceptional personality, hold the same authority over his former equals as a class officer does? And there the difference is slight. I am sure that no greater cause for discontent among the people could be found than by having Indians as civilians.

And last but not the least, there is the domiciled European population to be considered. What effect would it have on them if a large number of Indians were admitted to the administration? The answer is quite simple and was effectually given during the agitation over the Ilbert Bill in 1885—they would not stand it.

They are not too pleased with the present state of affairs, with the great power that lies in one man's hand, that of the head of the district. They chafe at it and are continually feeling and resenting its imperfections and limitations. They only submit to it because they see no way out of it and because he is English. Were he to be often an Indian they would resent it and make their resentment felt. They would lose the feeling of security they now have and they would not submit to this; they would make government impossible. To those who doubt their power to do this I would recommend a study of the agitation against the Ilbert Bill, more especially in its latest stages. It is no longer secret history that a disaster unequalled in Indian history was only saved at the last minute by the surrender of Government.

And the feelings which caused this are as vital now as then. It may be taken as an axiom that whatever Government might decree, the great British mercantile and other interests in India would refuse to allow any appreciable transfer of authority to the hands of Indians, and in face of their opposition it could not be done. That an Indian should rule Indians they would not mind perhaps, but that an Indian should rule Europeans, and that it should be to an Indian they looked for the maintenance of peace and order and for the administration of justice, criminal and civil, is unthinkable. The stability of the administration is due to its being English, and any threat to that stability would not be borne.

Besides, to what would it lead? Suppose, by a wild stretch of the imagination, all the Civil Service in India could be composed of Indians, what then? That is not self-government. The orders would still come from Downing Street, the responsibility rest with Parliament and the English people. The Government would not and could not so be Indianised; all that would have happened would be that a few hundred Indian gentlemen had been imperfectly Anglicised. Is that an ideal? Where would the three hundred and fifty million come in? No more than they do now. But in any self-government worth the name these people must come in; they must be the base on which the self-government is erected.

Government does not see its way. It must do something, and it has no idea what to do. A wise statesmanship would hold its hand till it saw clearly. But there is the danger that a hasty statesmanship may in despair do something for the mere sake of saying it is not standing still.

There is a way out of the present trouble, but I think it can be seen clearly enough that admitting Indians to the Civil Service is not that way. It might, in fact, be a very serious obstacle to following the right course.

India is lost, and will be regained by no such measures as those proposed. They will only deepen the gulf and accelerate the final rupture.

PART III
A NEW INDIA

CHAPTER XII

THE NEW CIVILIAN

India may be regained. How could that be done?

The first point is the *personnel* of the Indian Civil Service, which holds all important offices in India, forms the Government, and fills most of the places on the Indian Council at home.

It depends, as I have said, for its success not upon the ability, but on the personality of its members. India was achieved by personality and successfully governed by personality. It is personality alone that humanises rule and makes it tolerable, that stands between the people and rigid law, and can create that sentiment which alone binds ruler and ruled together.

How can that necessary personality be restored to it?

That this lack of personality does not affect only the Indian Civil Service is a matter of notoriety. It is exactly what our generals deplored after the Boer War—that the ordinary officer had no personality. It is a matter of common remark nowadays how exactly alike all the young men are, echoing sentiments that are not theirs. It is what the Germans say of us and the Americans, who especially admire and try to cultivate personality. We once stood before the world as a nation of personalities. We do so no longer.

To what is this due? Not to natural deficiency, because all children abound in personality. It is due to what is called "education." That too is no new discovery of mine, but a matter of common knowledge and publicity. Read, for instance, Harold Gorst's *The Curse of Education*. In Paine's *Life of Mark Twain*, systematic training is called "a blight." Neither is it a new thing. The Duke of Wellington said Waterloo was won in the playing-fields of Eton—not in the schools, be it noted. Yet in those days education was nothing like so rigid as it is now. Then take the notable Englishmen of the last fifty years; how few have been University men—many not public school men. Cobden and Bright, Chamberlain, Beaconsfield, Dickens and Kipling, Stanley, Captain Scott, and other pioneers of Empire, Huxley and Kelvin, all the great captains of industry. The two most prominent members of the Government to-day are not University men. Even where notable men were University men they did not attain their stature till they had thrown off its bonds. Gladstone was, for instance, the hope of the stern, unbending Tories till he had achieved his liberty, when he could think for himself. Yet even then he only achieved political, and never spiritual, freedom. Cecil Rhodes said that University dons were as children in some matters; meaning, however, ignorant and not ready to learn, which is not a child's attitude.

Therefore the fault lies with the "education."

What is Education?

There are two things that go to the proper upbringing of a child, and though they overlap in places they are distinct and even sometimes contradictory; one is Instruction, and the other is Education.

Reading and writing, arithmetic, and all information obtained from books or lectures or teachers is instruction; the bringing out of the powers of the child's own mind is education. The object of instruction is to enable the child to better his education. In itself it has no value. The mere acquirements of reading and writing—the mere accumulation of book knowledge—are in themselves worthless. "The learned fool is the biggest fool." They are only good insomuch as they help education.

What is education? It is the drawing out of a child's mind so that it can see life as it is, not a mere mass of phenomena, but a consequence of underlying causes; it is the exercising of his faculties of right judgment to meet events as they arise; it is an ability to gauge himself and others. Education is the cultivation of personality. It is to the child what careful gardening is to the tree—a help to growth so that it can develop its potentiality. The gardener helps each tree to put forth that essential quality of its own that differentiates it from all other trees and makes it a thing of use and beauty to the world. It is not a reduction to a common type or the standardisation of growth, because while the tree must harmonise with the rest of the garden it must have an individuality of its own.

That is education, and that alone is education. Instruction is simply providing the necessary food for growth, or giving the necessary weapons or implements to obtain that food. All instruction that does not directly tend to nourish personality is worse than waste—it occupies nerve and energy that are wanted for better things.

This is simple enough, yet the world is full of fallacies on the subject. Here is one from a well-known writer: "How can you draw out of a child a love for clean collars, Greek accents, the date of Bannockburn, or how to eat asparagus."

Well, you can only draw out a child's love for these things by helping him to see that the acquisition of them is a step towards a result the child desires to reach. Now Greek accents are only useful to a child who wishes to become a Greek tutor, and the date of Bannockburn is useful to no one because it can always be looked up if necessary; therefore no children have a taste for the latter, and not one in a thousand for the former. They are not education at all, and even as instruction they are worthless. A love of clean collars and how to eat asparagus can be drawn out of children by simply making them realise that unless they have their love for these things they will expose themselves to ridicule or contempt for no good purpose. For be it noted that until you do awaken this self-respect you will not get a child to put on clean collars enthusiastically, or be careful about asparagus. Instruction in such matters is useless—you must have education.

The man or woman properly educated will desire the right things, and will seek the right way of attaining these things. His actions will spring from a real living force within him. But if you teach him to do things because he is told or because it is the custom, you injure his personality; and as there is no driving force in a law or a custom, which are bonds, you confine him, whereas you should free him. It is an admission that he must not or cannot think for himself, but must blindly follow custom. It is true that he must, not only in boyhood but all through his life, yield obedience in act to persons, governments, or rules; but he must not do so blindly. It is a principal part of education to make the boy see for himself that such subordination of act is necessary to the progress of the world, because as individuals we can accomplish no great thing; then he will do it willingly, knowing its necessity. But it is equally necessary that the boy never subordinate his judgment to others, because any rule made absolute is death to progress, and there is no authority, nor rule, nor convention that should not be broken sometimes; and as time goes on all must be modified, changed, and relaxed; the ideal of education being that all authority will become unnecessary, as people will desire what is right, and do it *proprio moto*. The truth will have made them free.

Now seeing this difference, how much education is there in school or college? In the classrooms there is none. All that is given in classes is instruction, which may be useful or detrimental inasmuch as it helps personality or not. Usually it is detrimental, because it substitutes "authority" for insight. The child must accept something, not because he is helped to see that it is true, but because "somebody says so." Thus his personality is destroyed.

The only education he gets is in the playing-fields. There he learns to keep his temper, play the game, and co-operate, of his volition, with others to a desired end.

That is a valuable training, but it does not go very far. He is never taught to see life as it is for himself. On the contrary, he is forbidden to do so.

And this continues now till the age of twenty-two or twenty-three, so that by the time it is over the most receptive period of life is past. Bacon went to the University at thirteen, and left it at sixteen as he found it had no more to teach him.

Further, until some thirty or forty years ago a father considered that he owed some duty to his son—to help him, to lead him, to initiate him into life.

No one can do this but a father. No one can understand his son like a father and know what it is necessary for him to learn; to no one will the son listen, or confide in, as his father. But nowadays I notice that fathers have abdicated. They consider their duty fulfilled if they pay for the boy's schooling, and everything is left to the schoolmaster. Many fathers that I know are quite stranger to their sons. Mothers, on the contrary, strive more and more to obtain influence over their sons and bring them up in the principles of women. But a man must be a man or be nothing.

There is another and very considerable difference between schools now and the schools of sixty years ago and before. In the earlier period the schoolmasters were rarely clergymen; now they are practically always so; and not only that, but boys nowadays are far more under control and influence of their masters than they were.

Now whatever good points may be claimed for Church teaching by those who believe in it, there will, I think, be no difficulty about the admission that the frame of mind, the outlook on the world, of ecclesiastics is not suitable for men who have to lead an active life. It is, in fact, the very reverse of what a man requires whose first duty it is to understand the world and to lead the world. For to the ecclesiastic the world is a bad place, it has to be borne as best it can, to be condemned not understood, and all effort is directed not to this world but to some other. Moreover, the habit of thought of ecclesiastics is fixed. They believe that not only is truth absolute, but that they possess it or some of it; the very foundation-rock of their belief is authority, and freedom of thought is disliked by them as subversive of their tenets. Their principal qualities are those of submission, patience and obedience, not merely in act but in thought.

Now boys are apt to imitate their masters, and however secular a course of education may be, if it be given by ecclesiastics the boys are certain to be a great deal influenced by their master's outlook on life. That accounts for much of the pessimism that is observable, for the "unnatural mildness" of the modern young man. If you keep a boy under ecclesiastical habits of thought till he is twenty-three, how can he ever escape into the fresh air of free inquiry? How will he ever love the world instead of despising it? And no good work was ever done except by men who loved the world; and love comes from understanding, not from aloofness.

A boy's education should be directed from an early age towards the work he is to perform in life. What department of the public service is now held to be the best served? Is it not the Navy? And naval officers are caught young and trained *ad hoc*; not a narrow professional training, but none the less a training with an object. The present training of Indian civilians up till twenty-three is objectless, and therefore inefficient. That in the Army the special training is begun much later may account for the complaints of army officers wanting personality compared with naval officers.

With engineers and all specialised work the training begins young.

But the Indian civilian is ecclesiastically trained till he is twenty-three. Then he has to learn his work. Could there be a greater absurdity?

What then should be done?

In the first place he should be caught young. The work of the Indian civilian is as important to England as that of the sailor; it is even more specialised and difficult. He should be trained for it from fourteen or thereabouts, not from twenty-three.

It should be determined what special qualities are necessary for a good Indian civilian. I think some of them are obvious enough.

A good physique and a liking for sport.

Good manners and a knowledge of etiquette.

Discipline in act.

Freedom and courage in thought.

Knowledge of life and humanity as they are round him.

Let us consider these.

That physical fitness is the first necessity all will allow. The climate is severe and takes a great deal out of him, especially in the hot weather; there must be exposure in the districts; the work is hard and difficult, and makes great demands upon the physique. Therefore the physique must be good.

And a medical certificate of soundness is no guarantee of this. A man may be medically quite sound and yet so prostrated by the heat as to find his temper and his work affected. His physique lies at the base of all his work, and must be good. Nothing is now done to secure this; no investigation has ever been made as to the type that endures heat the best. Yet undoubtedly there is such a type. In that extraordinary book, *A Modern Legionary*, it is pointed out that in Tonquin, amongst the men of the Legion, a certain type stood the climate better than the others. Whenever any special service had to be performed it was men of a certain sanguine type that were chosen. Not that they were physically stronger or braver than the others, but because even in the greatest heat they retained a certain buoyancy of temperament which the darker types lost.

I have myself noticed something of the sort in Burma and India. Of course mere personal observation of this sort proves nothing, but the subject seems to deserve investigation. That all people do not bear heat and cold alike is undoubted. In the Russian campaign of 1812 it was the Italians who stood the cold best of all Napoleon's troops.

Anyhow, the cadet should have not merely a sound physique but a buoyant physique, and that cannot be ensured under the present system.

Then he should be made a good sportsman; for the Indian civilian no training is more necessary than this. I do not mean only a cricketer or football player; neither of these games is of much use out in the East. I mean a rider who is also fond of horses; a shot who is also interested in birds and animals.

There is in all sportsmen of this kind a quality which no one else has. I cannot define it. It comes, I think, from association with people out of his own rank in one pursuit, from having to go to them for knowledge he has not got himself and thereby recognising their value, from a subtle sympathy with nature as not apart from man, nor a setting for man, but another manifestation of the same Life that is in man. Nothing is more valuable in enabling a District Officer to keep his mind sweet. Official work is all concerned with the faults and shortcomings of others, wherein you are judge and they are culprits. Official work divides; it insensibly leads you to believe that all men are liars and robbers, and are trying to deceive you. Throw it aside, and go out to shoot, stopping in the villages talking of sport and village affairs, and the whole aspect of life changes. You wash off your priggishness; you cease to imagine yourself first cousin to the Deity; you return to your humanity, and with the first snipe you miss to your extreme fallibility.

Then there is ability at languages. Now although some men may develop an excess of ability to learn languages, all people have that ability to a certain extent when young or they could not learn their own language.

But it is an ability that quickly departs unless kept alive. The way Greek and Latin are taught is a sure way to destroy any ability for learning a language a boy may retain. Grammar should never be taught. No child learns its own language by grammar, and, in fact, grammar only applies to dead languages, not to living. That has to some extent dawned on modern educators, but I see that French grammar and regular and irregular verbs are taught to those learning French. Did Loti and Maupassant learn French grammar? I wonder. If not, why should anyone else? But schoolmasters are a hard lot, and there is no one who so absolutely refuses to learn as he who makes a profession of teaching. Why should not Hindustani be made the school language for Indian cadets?

Then come good manners. I do not mean only good English manners—those manners which enable you to pass in a meeting of cultivated English men and women—but much better manners than those. They are concerned with your conduct to your equals; but the only good manners that will be of much use to you in the East are those deeper manners which are equal to all occasions and can show an equal courtesy to a ploughman as to a peer, to an old Subadar hero of a hundred fights, to a headman and to a coolie. Some of it is, of course, convention and must be learned, like the right thing to do when an old soldier offers you the hilt of his sword, or a Burman lady brings you some fruit; but most of it, I think, simply comes from a frame of mind. If you recognise that the common humanity that binds you is eternal and that the difference of rank or race or age is a temporary difference that will pass, I do not think you will quite want for good manners. Orientals are particular about manners, and they do not respect a man who has none, or who has his own and not theirs.

Discipline in act is, I think, enough taught now, but freedom of thought is woefully to seek. It is banned by theology, and ecclesiastics naturally do not teach it.

As to knowledge of life, that can only come in the living. But it will not come unless you find the world worth studying and your own life worth living. If this world is bad, then it is not worth study, and if the only object of your life here is to fit you or unfit you for life in some spirit world, then you will not care much to fit yourself for this world.

Finally, it would appear too as if civilians should go out to India much younger than they do now. Twenty-three is far too old to begin a totally new life. For it must be remembered that life in India is a totally new life to which men have to get accustomed. No matter how you are trained in England, nothing will enable you to know India but being in India. The real education cannot begin until the student lands in the country in which he is to do his life's work. Everything he may learn at home is preliminary only. Language, people, work have all to be learned after arriving. However good the material provided may be, it is, when it lands, simply so much raw material. It has to learn everything. I do not think the age of twenty is at all too young to begin such a training; in fact I think nineteen would be better.

But we are now come to what should be done after arrival in India, and that will require a new chapter.

CHAPTER XIII

TRAINING IN INDIA (HIS TRAINING)

Having got the young civilian out to his province he should be thoroughly trained before being put to work, not given six or nine months to look round and then put to do work he cannot understand.

If he came out to India at twenty, he could well afford eighteen months or two years of real training.

During the cold weather he should be with some District Officer, accompanying him in camp, observing how he works, getting an insight into the mechanism of Government; during the hot weather he should be in the hills. By thus keeping him out of the great heat at the beginning he would become slowly acclimatised. Now he is plunged straight out from England into the Indian plains.

As to the training he should receive, that is not very difficult to suggest. First and foremost comes the language, of which a good colloquial knowledge should be required. It can only be acquired by talking to the people. A teacher is useful to explain difficulties encountered by a pupil in trying to talk, but no teacher can teach a language. In fact, languages cannot be taught—they can be acquired. The ability of the ear and vocal organs to recognise and reproduce strange sounds comes only with constant practice; and it must be practice with the people, for educated men talk differently from peasants in India as elsewhere. All Acts should be learned by first clearly understanding the principles that underlie them, the object sought to attain, and the method by which it is hoped to attain it. That is the only way to really understand an Act or Code. The detailed knowledge can be filled in later. In order to enable this to be done Government would have to frame introductions to their Codes and Acts. And such introductions would be most valuable not only to learners but to Government itself. Suppose, for instance, an introduction were written to the *Village Manual* explaining exactly what the village organism is and that the Act and Rules were intended to preserve and strengthen this organism; it would be immediately apparent that as they are now they really injure and destroy it. This would lead to a complete recast of the *Manual*—a most necessary work. And so with the other Acts and Rules. Now they are issued in a perfectly naked state that would be almost immodest had they any real life in them. But there is never any intention or life manifest, only dead formulæ. Such introductions would also be most valuable in keeping an Act up to date. A law may fairly fulfil its intention when issued, but as circumstances change it would become obvious that the Act was out of date. If however you don't know the intention of the Act, how are you to judge its relevancy?

Further, such introductions would prevent the abuse of certain sections. Did, for instance, the Government of India intend sections 109, 110, of the Criminal Procedure Code to be used as they are in Burma now? I doubt it. But Burma can always say: "How was I to know the intention? There are the sections. Why shouldn't I use them as I think fit?"

How would the imprisonment sections of the Civil Procedure Code be justified? What object are they supposed to attain? No one knows. It can't be to deter a man from being ruined—that is not necessary; it can't be to make him pay—the distraint sections are for that; it can't be to render him a better citizen—gaols don't do that. What are they for, then? To pander to the creditors' desire for vengeance? It can only be that. I would like to see Government avow it.

Then the young civilian should get an insight into the customs of the people and learn to understand what these customs mean. Nothing is more absurd than the way ceremonies are misinterpreted, not merely by the casual observer, but by what is called "science." A whole theory of "marriage by capture" has been built on ceremonies that are symbolical, not of an absurdity like that, but of certain facts of human nature common to all marriages in all periods all over the world. The Nairs of Malabar have been credited with the most extraordinary forms of polyandry on the strength of ceremonies which were adopted as a protection to deceive the Brahmins. Human nature is, in its essentials, always the same. If the learner is helped to look under ceremonies he will see this. A knowledge of ceremonies has its value, like a knowledge of clothes has; but as clothes are used for good reasons—sometimes to hide the form, sometimes to accentuate parts of the form—so are ceremonies. And ceremonies may and do persist long after the human need has left them.

Further, he should know something of the economic state of the people. I think that a District Officer should be acquainted with the principal industries of his district, so as to be able to give help if need be. Generally speaking, the help he can give is protection from rash innovations. The cultivator neither in India nor in Burma is blind to his own interest, nor is he ignorant. He has behind him an experience of thousands of years, which have taught him a great deal about the capability of crops and soils. But he is quite willing to learn more, only he must make sure first. He cannot afford to experiment. His system will give him a living, and a change may mean starvation. He cannot run the risk. Prove to him that a new crop will grow and will fetch a decent price, and he is eager to cultivate it; but nothing less than ocular proof will do. That is, of course, right. He has common sense.

Unfortunately, not everyone has so much sense, and there are continual attempts being made to get him to make experiments he cannot afford. He should be protected against these. I can remember two such attempted booms in Upper Burma, both engineered by Government—one was cotton, and one was coffee or tea planting.

The cotton boom was very rigorously pressed upon us from England because I believe someone in authority had promised to "take his coat off" to make it succeed. But Burma is not a good cotton country, and the long staple will not grow. Moreover, if it could be grown with irrigation it would not pay nearly so well as rice. Therefore the cultivator will have none of it.

Tea and coffee planting is only suitable for capitalists, not for peasants; and as a matter of fact coffee won't grow north of about 12° north latitude. So these booms fizzled out, but they created a good deal of trouble first.

Indeed, most of my experiences were putting dampers on enthusiasts, Government or other, who wanted something grown, and who were ready to affirm that if it would not grow it ought to grow and must be made to grow, and sell afterwards as well. I remember a correspondence I had with a gentleman in Lower Burma on the subject of a fibre-producing plant which is grown in small patches near the villages of my district to serve as string. This gentleman heard of the plant and wrote to me a glowing account of the future before it, strongly urging me to advise my people—nay, to force my people—to grow it in large quantities for export. I wrote back that if he was so interested in the matter he should come up to my district and enter into contracts with the villagers to grow it for him. They would, I knew, do it at a certain price which I gave, and I offered to help him in every way. He, however, indignantly refused. He was not a trader, and the villagers should grow it on speculation. As it happens, I have a considerable knowledge of fibre plants gained before I entered Government service, and as I knew there was no certain market for this fibre I let well alone.

But most of all, I think a young officer should learn that it is not only for the people's pleasure but for his own pleasure and for the good of Government that he should encourage the amusements of the people. Nothing will give him more influence than this, make him better known, or cause his official work to go so easily.

It is a continual complaint among the people now that life is so dull. Our administration has not only taken all the adventure and picturesqueness out of life, but it has been disastrous to sport. Boat-racing, for instance, which used to be a great sport all along the Irrawaddy, is now nearly dead, and amateur dancing troupes which used to be common in the villages are nearly all defunct. I believe they are *all* dead. Now this is a disastrous state of things. Man wants play as well as work, and if he can't get amusement he will do things he shouldn't. The principal reason given for this decay is that unless some high official will interest himself in sports and give them his encouragement, no one will get them up. Therefore, when I was in Sagaing I instituted a regatta in the October holidays. It was no trouble to me. Directly I said I would like to have races there were plenty of well-known Burmans ready to do all the work with pleasure and enthusiasm.

The riverside villages caught up the idea. They pulled out their old racing canoes and did them up anew. Crews were put into training, and for weeks all the talk was of times and spurts and the merits of this crew and that. Sagaing didn't know itself.

The races duly came off in the glorious full-moon week of October, when all Courts are closed for ten days and everyone has holidays. Many crews came, and their friends and relatives came, and their supporters and backers, and they brought their wives and sisters with them. In the evenings we had boat races, at night we had pagoda festivals and dances and illuminations.

All went well till the final great event, which was a race between our champion boat and a boat sent over from Mandalay to challenge us.

There was immense excitement about this because the Mandalay boat was said to be a swagger boat; but then so was ours, a very swagger boat. Mandalay bet on their boat. Sagaing laid their rupees on the Sagaing boat; and the banks on both sides the mile-wide river were thronged with spectators. Then a catastrophe occurred. Just before the race our steersman was discovered drunk and happy upon the beach. How this happened I don't know. Why the crew ever allowed him to be separated from them I can't think; and his own explanation threw no clear light on the subject. He said in self-defence that the enemy in disguise had lured him into a toddy shop and "must have hocussed the toddy, for I only had a couple of cups, yet see me now," and there was great indignation. Whether in consequence of his defection or not I don't know, but we lost. Mandalay just romped away from us, and not only secured the prize, but was declared to have carried off a "cart-load" of rupees won in bets.

However, notwithstanding that disaster the meeting was a great success, and now, after ten years, that is the principal event I remember of my three years' administration. It stands out in my memory, and I think that probably if the people ever remember me at all it is as the convener of the first regatta for many years.

There was an amusing sequel to this defeat by Mandalay. For months afterwards whenever I had an insolvent case in my Court the debtor attributed his failure to this race. The district was "stony broke" in consequence, at least so the insolvents in my Court said. The conversation would run as follows:

The Judge (myself).	Well, I have read your schedule, and you are five hundred rupees out. How is that? Explain.
Debtor.	I am a honest man, your Honour, and never in debt before.
Myself.	No doubt. How did it happen this time?
Debtor.	Well, your Honour will remember that last October your Honour got up boat races here.
Myself.	Certainly.
Debtor.	And Mandalay sent us a challenge.
Myself.	Well?
Debtor.	Naturally I believed in *our* boat. (Note the "our"—his and mine). I was sure it must win, and for our [his and my] credit I wagered all I could get on it.

Myself.	Hum!
Debtor.	We lost.
Myself.	There was always a possibility of that.
Debtor (indignantly).	Not with a fair race. But they drugged our steersman. I call it a swindle, but I had to pay, and consequently am now insolvent and in your Honour's hands.

Was there any truth in this? There was no truth, of course. These debtors became insolvent through the action of two or three newly arrived firms of money-lenders. That was clear enough. Possibly they had a rupee or two on the boat race, but that would hardly affect matters. They made this appeal to try to get at me—the man—behind the law in which I was encased. They will do anything to achieve that. Like all human beings they are terrified at law and want to touch humanity, no matter what it does. They can bear from a man what they cannot from a law. This is manifest all through one's official life. People, for instance, will not come to see you in Court, but come to your private house. That is to try to get at the humanity they know you possess. That is what they want—your personality; for it will understand; whereas a law—what can it know of anything?

Then there are the dancing troupes for girls. What other amusements have girls but these troupes? They love them. Many girls have told me that it was the practising for the dances which gave a meaning and an interest to their girlhood. It taught them what lessons could never do—grace and elocution and style. It collected the villagers together; it gave a village something to be proud of. There should be such troupes in all big villages, and when the village system is restored there will be no doubt a renaissance of these and other amusements.

Again, why should not there be village teams of football? The Burmans like the game immensely, and play it well. But of course for village play the rules would have to be greatly simplified. They are too scientific now. It should be a game.

Thus it seems to me a District Officer should be educated to be the head of his district in all ways, not merely its judge or its schoolmaster. His other work must be lightened. Much of the work he does should not be done at all. All interference with the village should cease. If the suggestions I have to make in a later chapter as to self-government were adopted, the District Officer would soon feel the relief. He now seeks for work to do. He should try to avoid work as much as he can. "Don't interfere, except where you must," should be his rule. Now it is the other way about. And Government should regard him quite differently from what it does now. It should trust him, and not law. He must work within law, but not by law. When he has something to decide he should consider what is the right and proper thing to do, and then see if he can legally do it. If not, he must modify his order till it is within law. Now he looks to the law to tell him what to do. That is bad. Laws are bonds, not guides. They cannot give you motive force. They tell you what not to do, and that is all.

He should be trusted far more than he is. He should not be made to "fall into line." He should be judged not by his acts, but by the result of his acts, or his refusals to act, that is, by the state of his district. He should not be transferred when it can be helped, but be encouraged to make long stays in a district. He will do so if you give him a free hand so that he can take a personal interest in his work and people. The secret of success is personality.

I think if the young men sent out were trained on these or some such lines there would soon be a very different feeling between people and Government from what there is now. There would be a mutual understanding and respect which are now lacking.

There is a further suggestion I have to make as regards District Officers, not for their training, but for regulating their relations to the Government above them. They should be consulted prior to all legislation that affects their districts.

It will, of course, be said that they are now so consulted. Drafts of new Acts or amendments of Acts are sent round for comment and criticism, and so District Officers are consulted.

I don't call that consultation; even if it come within the dictionary meaning of the word it does not come within its spirit.

Take a concrete case: Suppose a new Village Act to be drafted and sent round to District Officers for criticism, how can any one officer criticise it effectively, or make useful suggestions, except by chance? His experience is confined to one, or two, or three districts; the Act is for the Province. He may make suggestions to suit his district; he cannot tell if they will suit others. He has no idea why certain provisions are included. He has no certain basis for constructive criticism. Very often he won't criticise at all. He says: "What is the use? It's only sent to me as a matter of form." Besides, as I have pointed out, the opinions of a number of individuals taken one by one differ greatly from the opinion of the same number sitting together and discussing various points of view before framing an opinion.

But what Government wants is the collective opinion of its District Officers, and not many varying views. It would have far more confidence in such an opinion, and be more careful in disregarding it. Why should not District Officers meet once a year to discuss pending questions, to consider new Acts, to suggest changes in old Acts? Their proceedings would, of course, be private, and not for publication. Officers should be encouraged to speak out. It would be a great help to all of them, and I think it would give Government a sense of security it has not got now.

CHAPTER XIV

OTHER SERVICES

The Indian Civil Service is the principal service in India; it furnishes men for the executive, the magistracy, and judicature, the revenue administration; and its members constitute not only the Local Government, but, excepting for the Law member and one or two others, the Council of the Government of India. Therefore it is in every way the most important service to have in harmony with the people. It is not, however, the only service manned by Englishmen, and it is very necessary that the other services also should be efficient. These are the Forest Department, the Engineer Department, and the Police. Of the first two I have nothing to say. They are technical departments, and although of course I have had a good deal to do with them, only a member of their own department would have the specialist knowledge to criticise them. I believe they are dissatisfied, but how far their grievances can be rectified I don't know.

With the police it is different. Though a separate department, they work in close touch with the District Magistrate, who is, in fact, their legal head. He must be intimately acquainted with their working, and with his Superintendent of Police personally in order that work in the district may go easily.

The first requisite for a good police-officer is a knowledge of the language. It is even more necessary for him than for the civilian. It is an absolute essential. And in the men of my day it was an essential that was fulfilled for the most part. Whether it will be so with the men enlisted under the new system of competitive examination in England is more doubtful. The men of former days entered the service younger, and the receptivity of their minds for acquiring languages had not been destroyed by "education." It is, I think, a pity that a competitive examination has been made the entrance-gate to the police. Such examinations prove nothing good in those who pass them. They may be good men, but preparation for examination has not increased that goodness.

I do not believe in competitive examinations. For instance, take the Indian Police; what qualities are required in a good Superintendent of Police? They are ability to command, facility in two languages at least, tact, a knowledge of human nature. What does an examination select him for? Ability in any of these? No, but for a retentive memory of written words such as Greek or Latin, for dry rules such as grammar, for memory of dry and useless facts such as history as it is taught, for mathematics. Is there any obvious connection between these two sets of qualities? There is none whatever. Has experience shown that ability in the first argues ability in the second? Experience shows the reverse.

Neither is the athletic ability for which marks are given to Rhodes scholars any test whatever of anything but itself. Without wishing for a moment to infer that athletic ability argues a deficiency in mental ability, I would ask how many of the leaders the world has known were great athletes? Nelson, or Lord Roberts, or Napoleon, for instance. Whenever ability of muscle and of brain have occurred together it has been incidental, not causal. Muscular ability is a good thing, but there are better things.

Success in competitive examinations proves one thing only—that the candidate has a good memory for words. It very frequently follows that he is unable to go beneath words, and that he puts his trust in words and papers and formulæ because the habit of mind set up by examinations tends to this.

There is no sense in these examinations for anyone, except perhaps for those about to be tutors of the same things. Men of action and scholars are different in grain and the test for one usually eliminates the other. That there are a few exceptions only demonstrates that human nature cannot be confined within hard and fast rules. But there can be successful generalisation.

Competitive examinations are a fetish which Government worships because it is afraid of taking the responsibility of appointing officers on its own initiative. It is afraid of the charge of nepotism. But it would not be nepotism to give the sons of its officers, Civil and Military, first chance of appointments in the Police. It would be a graceful recognition of the fact that when a man has spent his life in India he has lost touch with England and cannot get his sons placed at home, therefore he deserves consideration for them from the Government he has served. I do not believe in heredity in such matters because there is no evidence in its favour; but I do believe in early associations and traditions. Now the traditions and associations of the sons of officers who have served in India are with India.

I believe that a much sounder way would be to appoint sons of officers who have served in India. They have Indian traditions, and, what is more, having as children learned the language it soon returns to them.

I know this as a fact. Some twenty-five years ago in Upper Burma a young police-officer was sent to the same station with me in Burma. He came direct from India, but had been born and brought up in Burma till he was seven, when he went to England to school. From England, at eighteen or nineteen, he went to India—the Punjab, I think—and was appointed to the Police there. When Upper Burma was in need of officers he was sent to Burma on promotion. On arrival he did not remember a word of Burmese, but it came rapidly back to him. When sitting with me when I was talking to the Burmese he would continually say to me, "Didn't you say so-and-so?" and "Didn't he answer so-and-so?" Without learning it, his memory recalled the language to him, and in a month or two he was talking it well and with a good accent.

There remain the Subordinate Civil Service and the Lower Grades of the Police, all or nearly all of whom are native to the Province.

In another book, writing on this subject, I said: "I read and hear continually that many of our native magistrates and judges and police are corrupt. I am told they take bribes, that they falsify cases, that they make right into wrong. I wish to say that I have no belief in such charges. Exceptions there may be, but that the mass of our Burman fellow-officers are honest I have no doubt." All my experience has tended to support that view.

Everyone in the world requires looking after, requires check and supervision, requires that protection between himself and harm that only a watching eye can give, and in Burma, for the Burmese officials, these safeguards hardly exist.

It must be remembered that official Burma has no Press to criticise it, no native society to give it tone, no organised community to help the individual in the right path. He has many temptations, and a fall is easy.

I do not believe in the general charge that Burmese are corrupt. That occasional cases of undue influence should occur is natural if you consider the circumstances under which they serve. They are not, like the English officers, independent of their surroundings in social matters. They have, for company's sake, to associate with the pleaders, the merchants, the headmen, and others within their charge. Their families are with them, and they are interested in the happenings of the town or village, and are concerned in it. They are inevitably influenced in many ways, which we do not appreciate. They know things which we do not. In cases that come before them they often know of events behind the scenes which lead up to the final happening which comes into Court. It is useless to say that they should not be influenced by anything but the evidence on the record; they cannot help being influenced. They have, for instance, known of A being a trouble to his parents long before the charge which they have to try, and that is in their minds; or they know B to be a good character, and that his accusers are doubtful people. It has happened to me, not once but many times, that on appeal I have read a judgment of a Burmese Subordinate Magistrate which puzzled me, because, though not contrary to the evidence, there has evidently been in the writer's mind something more than the evidence. In such cases I have usually inquired personally from the magistrate what it was he knew before passing orders on appeal, and I have sometimes taken further evidence on that point so as to get the record straight. It is easy to say that magistrates should not be affected by anything but the recorded evidence, just as it is easy to say that a magistrate should be blind. Magistrates are human beings—fortunately.

But, of course, the standard might be higher. This raising of the standard can, however, only be attained by raising the standard of independence in the people, and our rule tends to decrease this. Under self-government it will rise. It is self-government and its consequent publicity which have purified Courts in England. Look at Judge Jeffreys and his time. We are not people to adopt too Pharisaic an attitude.

Elsewhere I have commented on the failure of the "educated" native to make a good official, and I need not repeat myself. The education we give is not good for them, but until a national system of education is instituted I don't see what we can do. The subordinate service, as long as it is subordinate, cannot attract the best men, because the prospects are poor.

As to the rank and file of the police I have this to say—they are unsatisfactory, and the Police Commission did not get at the real causes. Do Commissions ever get at real causes? Are they not merely excuses to give "face" to Government? What is the use of examining innumerable witnesses none of whom have probed the subject? Answers to difficult questions are not got by asking, but by personal experience: by a man or men capable of understanding what they see and finding out the causes.

Pay has something to do with the poorness of the material, but in Burma at least it is not the principal cause. That cause is that the police are disliked, and they are disliked because they are part of a legal system which is disliked and disapproved of. The police are considered almost as enemies of the people. To rehabilitate the police and get really good men into it the whole criminal system requires amendment. When the people like and admire the Courts they will like and will enter the service of those Courts. Now they will do neither. A popular Government may be a good Government; an unpopular Government cannot possibly be so.

Further, it is said that the Burman takes badly to discipline and will never, therefore, make a good policeman nor soldier.

That he takes badly to discipline is true, but what is the reason? That he is essentially different from other people? That is absurd. The reason of it lies in his past history, his environment and education.

When we took Upper Burma it was hardly an organised nation at all. It was only a mass of villagers which acknowledged a king over all. There was no national army—because no need for one—and no large industries. The Burman has been a free man and he has the religion—or want of religion—of a free man. He has never had priests to rule him, to force on him reverence and obedience as virtues, to destroy his individuality. Therefore he has lived free. And nowadays, although he is lectured enough on his want of discipline, the advice is given in the wrong way and apropos of the wrong subject.

He ought in the opinion of his critics to be a good policeman or a good soldier, or a good employé for the rice merchants in Rangoon, and he is not. Therefore he is lectured on his want of discipline. "That is to say," thinks the Burman, "I am lectured and abused in order that I may be a more useful tool in the hands of a foreign Government, or a more profitable servant to a foreign merchant—who will reap the benefit."

That is what he thinks and rightly thinks, for the advice is so prompted and so meant.

He has yet to learn that discipline in act is necessary to enable him to attain his own ideals, to create and maintain his own self-government, and to establish industries that will compete with the foreigner's. He must himself establish organisms in order to succeed.

The Burman is afraid of discipline, partly because it is new to him, and partly because he is afraid that by surrendering independence of act he will surrender independence of spirit.

This can only be got over by a true education, by making the boy see for himself that only in union is strength, and that he must learn to act with others, and therefore under leaders. He will see this fast enough if it is carefully shown him when young. He will accept it also if it is clearly demonstrated to him that obedience in act does not infer surrender of his soul. It is the latter he is afraid of, and wisely. Tell him that not only may he think for himself, but that he is bound to do so, while at the same time subordinating private opinions to a common end, and you will get discipline as much as you like. It is a matter of common sense, and he has plenty of that.

The mechanical obedience to masters and spiritual or material pastors because they have been "set in authority" over us should never be taught. They have not been set in authority. They may deserve obedience if they are leaders in the right way, and we should co-operate with them there by serving them towards an end good for both. Get the boy to understand that. Then you get that willing and intelligent obedience which is worth all the mechanical obedience in the world. This is true in all walks of life. If you wish to read of a startling example, read of how the Revolutionary troops of France, as soon as they had gained a little experience, met and overthrew the wooden and lifeless battalions of Prussia, which had been drilled to death.

There must be life and intelligence, and a purpose in obedience as in all else for it to be a virtue. In itself obedience is not an end, it is only justifiable as a means to an end. It must arise from the exercise of will, not from its atrophy or from surrender to the will of others. You obey because you wish to obey, not because you are forced to do so.

That is the true education in discipline.

But all this can only come with local self-government, local patriotism, and a national education. They are what make a nation.

CHAPTER XV

LAW REFORM

When the *personnel* of the Government of India from the bottom to the top has been reorganised on a basis of understanding of the people, it will begin to revise its laws, and the first will be its Penal Law, its Criminal Courts and Procedure.

To do this with any success it will be necessary first to study the causation of crime, because until you know how it is caused you cannot possibly frame any system of prevention that is likely to do less harm than good.

This is a subject that many men have been studying for some years past, but very little progress has yet been made. The old shibboleths that crime results from a desire for crime and that the only cure is savage punishment still hold good with all Governments, though quite discredited outside official circles. It is a most fascinating subject, and as it is one I have worked at for many years I may be excused for devoting a somewhat large space to it here.

It is more than twenty-five years ago that my attention was first attracted to the causation of crime. I was a young magistrate then, trying my first cases; very nervous, very conscientious that I should fulfil all the legal requirements as laid down in the Codes. It had never occurred to me then that there was any gulf between justice and law—I supposed that they were one, that law was only codified and systemised justice; therefore, in fulfilling the Law I thought that I was surely administering Justice.

I was trying a theft case. I cannot remember now what it was that had been stolen, but I think it was a bullock. The accused was undefended, and I, as the custom is, questioned him about the case, not with the view of getting him to commit himself, but in order to try to elicit his defence, if any. He had none. He admitted the theft, described the circumstances quite fully and frankly, and said he was guilty. I asked him if he knew when he took the bullock from the grazing ground that he was stealing it, and he answered "Yes." I asked him if he knew that the punishment for cattle theft was two years' imprisonment, which practically meant ruin for life, and he replied that he knew it would be heavy.

Then I asked, "Why did you do it?"

He moved uneasily in the dock without answering, looked about him, and seemed puzzled.

I repeated the question.

Evidently he was trying to remember back why he had done it, and found it difficult. He had not considered the point before, and introspection was new to him. "Why did I do it?" he was saying to himself.

"Well?" I asked.

He looked me frankly in the face. "I don't know," he said. "I suppose I could not help it. I did not think about it at all; something just made me take it."

He was convicted, of course, and I forgot the case.

But I did not forget what he had said. It remained in my mind and recurred to me from time to time, I did not know why. For I had always been taught that crime was due to an evil disposition which a person could change, only he would not, and I had as yet seen no reason to question this view. Therefore the accused's defence appealed to no idea that was consciously in my mind. I did not reflect upon it. I can only suppose that, unconsciously to myself, these words reached some instinct within me which told me that they were true. And at last from the very importunity of their return I did begin to think about them, and, consequently on them, of the causation of crime in general. A curiosity awoke which has never abated, has indeed but grown, as in some small ways I was able to satisfy it.

What causes crime? Is it a purely individual matter? If so, why does it follow certain lines of increase or decrease, or maintain an average? That looks more like general results following on general causes than the result of individual qualities. Why is it not curable? It should have been cured centuries ago. Why does punishment usually make the offender worse instead of better? If his crime were within the individual's control, its punishment certainly would deter. It does not. Any deterrent effect it may have is rarely on him who is punished, but on the outside world, and that is but little. So much I saw very clearly in practice, and every book I read on the subject confirmed this. The infamous penal laws of England a hundred years ago did not stop crime; flogging did not stop garotting, it ceased for other causes. I began to think and to observe.

Some three years later my attention was still more strongly drawn to this subject.

I was then for a short time the Governor of the biggest gaol in the world, that in Rangoon. It was crowded with prisoners under sentence for many different forms of crime, from murder or "dacoity"—that is gang robbery—to petty theft.

The numbers were abnormal, and they were so not only here, but in all the gaols of both the Upper and Lower Provinces. The average of crime had greatly risen.

Why was this?

The reason was obvious. The annexation of the Upper Province six years before had caused a wave of unrest, not only there, but in the delta districts as well, that found its expression in many forms of crime. There was no doubt about the cause. But this cause was a general cause, not individual. The individual criminals there in the gaol did not declare the war. That was the consequence of acts by the King of Burma and the Government of India controlled by the English Cabinet, and was consequent on acts of the French Government. Therefore half of these individuals had become criminals because of the disagreements of three Governments, two of which were six thousand miles away from Rangoon.

There is no getting out of that. In normal times the average of convicts would have been only half what it was. The abnormality was not due to the convicts themselves.

Thus if A and B and C were suffering punishment in the gaol the fault is primarily not theirs. A special strain was set up from without which they could not stand and they fell.

But if this is true of half the prisoners, why not of the other half? There was no dividing line between the two classes. Political offences apart, you could not walk into the gaol and, dividing the convicts into two parts, say: "The crimes of this half being due to external causes, they must be pardoned; the crimes of the other half being due to their own evil disposition, they must continue to suffer." There was no demarcation.

Therefore, general causes are occasionally the cause of crime. Here was a long step in advance.

Again, four years later I was on famine duty in the Upper Province, and the same phenomenon occurred. There was an increase in certain forms of crime. Thefts doubled. Other crimes such as cheating and fraudulent dealings with money decreased. Here was again a general cause. Half of those thieves would have remained honest men all their lives, been respected by their fellow-men, and, according to religions, have gone to heaven when they died, but for the famine.

The causes of the famine were want of rain acting on the economic weakness of the people reared by the inability of government. Thus, had rain fallen as usual, had the people been able to cultivate other resources, had government been more advanced and experienced, half these thieves would not have been in gaol; and no one knew which half, for thefts of food did not increase. There was, in fact, no reason they should, as Government provided on the famine camps a subsistence wage for everyone who came.

On the other hand, certain individuals were saved from misappropriating money, or cheating in mercantile transactions, because there was little money left to misappropriate and not much business. If they lived honestly and went to heaven, the chief cause would be the failure of rain that year, not any superior virtue of their own. But no one knew who these individuals were who were so luckily saved.

But when you have acknowledged this, what is becoming of the doctrine of individual responsibility for crime? If a man has complete free-will to sin or not, if crime be due to innate wickedness, how does want of rain bring this on? And where is the common sense or common justice in punishing him for what is really due to a defective climate? He cannot control the rain. Manifestly then, as regards at least half of these thieves, there was no innate desire to steal, because that could not be affected by the famine. Had they desired to be thieves they would have been so in any case. The truth is that they did not desire to be thieves, but when the famine increased the temptation, and, through physical weakness, decreased their power of resistance, they fell. They sinned—not through spiritual desire of evil, but through physical inability to resist temptation.

But if this is true of half, why not of the whole? There is no line of demarcation. If true of some crime, why not of all? The doctrine of a man's perfect free-will to sin or not to sin as he pleases is beginning to look shaky. It will be as well to consider it.

What is free-will?

There is no necessity to discuss the meaning of "free"; we all know it; there is nothing ambiguous about it; but with "will" it is different. There are few words so incessantly misused as this word "will." Philosophers are the worst offenders, and the general public but follow their blind lead; yet unless you know exactly what you mean by it how can you use it as a counter of your thought?

What does *will* mean? "Where there's a will there's a way"—what does this mean? Does it mean wish? If, for instance, you are poor and stupid, can any quantity of wish make you rich? If you are weak will it make you strong? If you have no ear will it make you a musician? If you are a convict can it liberate you? That is absurd.

"Will," then means more than wish; to the desire must be added the ability—actual or potential. That is evident, is it not? Without the ability the wish avails nothing.

"Will," then, has two complements, both of which are necessary to it. Its meaning is not simple but compound; never forget this; never suppose that merely wishing with all your power can produce "will." It cannot unless the ability be developed to aid it.

And now we get back from words to human nature—Is the criminal so because he wants to be so? No, and No, and No again. No such wicked fallacy was ever foisted upon a credulous world as this. Nobody at any period of the world ever wished to be criminal. Everyone instinctively hates and fears crime; everyone is honest by nature; it is inherent in the soul. I have never met a criminal that did not hate his crime even more than his condemners hate it. The apparent exceptions are when a man does not consider his act a crime; he has killed because his victim exasperated him to it; he has robbed society because society made war on him. The offender hates his crime.

"But he is not ashamed of it."

Now that is true. He is not ashamed of it in the current sense. He hates it; he fears it; but it does not fill him with a sense of sin.

"Therefore," says the purist, "he has a hardened conscience. It is his conscience, as I said, that is at fault."

But the purist is wrong. He does not understand the criminal. He has never tried to understand him as I have tried. What the criminal feels towards his crime is what the sick man feels towards the delirium that seizes him—what the "possessed of devils" feels towards the possession when it comes. It terrifies him; he knows he must succumb; he fears not the mere penalty, but the crime. But he is not ashamed, because he knows he cannot help it. And punishment exasperates him because he has not deserved it, and it will do him harm, not good. He wants to be cured—not made a fit dwelling for still worse devils. And that is what punishment does.

The effect of punishment in deterring a criminal from repeating his crime is small. All study of criminal facts proves this. It generally makes him more prone to crime, not less; and all the great crimes are committed by men who have been still further ruined in gaols. What good effect punishment may have is mainly exercised on other than the criminal.

Punishment has some effect, but how much we do not yet know, because the matter has never been investigated, and it is not on the patient. Crime is a disease, and will you stop a fever by punishing the patients? Whatever good gaols do lies in the fact that they isolate the unhealthy from the healthy and so stop for a time infection, as do hospitals with disease. But the hospitals do not discharge the patient till he is cured; the gaol aggravates the liability to the disease and turns out the sufferer worse than before.

Let us go back. A man is criminal not because he wishes to be so, but because he cannot resist the temptation. He lacks will. True, but it is the ability he lacks, not the wish. Why does he lack ability?

This brings us to the second theory of crime—a new one—that criminals are born, not made. The tendency to crime is said to be inherent, to be a reversion, to be inherited. That explains why it is generally incurable when once contracted.

Many books have been written on this, but one fallacy vitiates them all. The observers have not observed the criminal in the making but when made. They have assumed the criminal to be of a race apart, and so founded their house upon the sand. Lombroso went so far as to lay down certain stigmata that inferred a criminal disposition. The stigmata have been shown to be universal, and there is no such thing as a "criminal disposition." If there be other qualities that do differentiate the criminal from the normal man, they are not innate.

That those born crippled in some way frequently become criminals is no exception; it denotes no criminal disposition. But the cripple is handicapped in the struggle for life. He is cut off from the many pleasures of work and play, of love and children, which his fellows have. He is sensitive and he is jeered at and despised. Is it any wonder that under such circumstances he becomes sometimes embittered? A cripple is set apart from his fellow-men. There are for him but two alternatives—to be a saint or a criminal. Love and care and training will make him a saint; neglect too often makes him a criminal. But to whom the blame for the latter? Not to him.

Connected with this theory is the supposition that criminality is hereditary.

There are few subjects on which so much "scientific" nonsense is talked and written as this of heredity. Not very much is known of it as regards plants, less of animals, and almost nothing as regards humanity. Furthermore, the experience gained in plants and animals is useless as regards humanity. Evolution in humanity tends to greater brain power, but all cultivation in animals and plants has tended to destroy brain power and even adaptability. To read books on heredity is to read a mass of suppositions and hazardous inductions where most of the facts are negative and the exceptions are positive. There is nothing so easy and nothing so fatal as this tendency to attribute to heredity what is due to training, or want of training. It excuses supineness in Governments and professions. Here is what John Stuart Mill, a profound thinker, thought of this facile recourse to heredity as an excuse:

"Of all vulgar methods of escape from the effects of social and moral influences on the mind, the most vulgar is that of attributing the diversions of conduct and character to inherent natural differences."

This, too, is what Buckle said: "We often hear of hereditary talents, hereditary vices, and hereditary virtues; but whoever will critically examine the evidence will find that there is no proof of their existence. The way in which they are usually proved is in the highest degree illogical; the usual course being for writers to collect instances of some mental peculiarity found in a parent and his child, and then to infer that the peculiarity was bequeathed. By this mode of reasoning we might demonstrate any proposition. But this is not the way in which the truth is discovered; and we ought to enquire not only how many instances there are of hereditary talents, etc., but how many instances there are of such qualities not being hereditary."

I have for myself, neither in life nor in books, found one single case in which it could be confidently said that a criminal weakness was inherited. That A, a criminal, has a son B, who also became criminal, proves nothing. You must first prove that a similar child of different stock would not become criminal if brought up as A's son was. You must also prove that if you took away A's son as a child and brought him up differently he would still show criminal weakness. But all the facts negative this. The child even of a criminal tribe in India, if removed from its environment, grows up like other children. Coming of criminal ancestors has not handed down a criminal aptitude. You must not mistake inheritance of other traits for inheritance of criminal aptitudes. A is very quick-tempered, which he has not from a child been trained to control. Under sudden provocation he kills a man. His son B inherits his father's quick temper, is similarly badly brought up, and the same thing occurs. The hasty hereditary theorist says: "Behold the inheritance of a propensity to murder." But quick temper is not a criminal trait; it is often an accompaniment of the kindest disposition. It is an excess of sensitiveness. The training, physical and mental, was in each case lacking, and a coincidence of provocation caused a coincidence of crime.

Let it be once clearly discerned that if a quality be hereditary it is always hereditary, and cannot appear, except as the result of heredity—and the absurdity of modern theories will be manifest.

There is not—there has never been in anyone—a tendency to crime until either gaols or criminal education creates it. No one ever wanted to commit crime as crime. A daring boy with no outlet for his energy may break out into violence, robbery, and later into burglary; he would not have done so had his physical need for exercise and his spiritual need for facing danger had another outlet. The instincts that led him into crime were good and noble instincts which, finding no legitimate channel, found an illegitimate channel for themselves.

In that fine book of Mr. Holmes', entitled *London's Underworld,* is an account of how hooligans are made. The young men are full of energy—they want exercise, struggle, the fight of the football field or the hockey match, and they cannot get it. They have no playground but the streets and no outlet for their energy save hooliganism. The pity of it!

What, then, causes crime?

It is never the wish for crime. It is one of two causes. Either it is the only outlet for some natural instinct which is denied legitimate outlet by the environment, or it is due to an inability to resist temptation when it offers.

How can it be prevented?

Now this inability is physical. The wish is spiritual—the ability is physical and depends greatly on health. With ill-health or malnutrition in the young the first thing to give is the power of control. The average of criminals are a stone underweight. Therefore, crime is dependent to a great extent on health. Ill-health causes crime; accidental mutilation causes crime; accident creates an aptitude to crime; neglected youth and education cause crime.

Religion does not affect crime one way or another. The greatest criminals are often religious. Mediæval Europe was very religious and very criminal, and there are many other instances. Honesty is inborn in all; it is part of the "light that lighteth every man that is born into this world"; it requires no teaching. What must be acquired is the ability to give effect to it. Crime is a physical, not a spiritual disease. And crime is no defect of the individual. It is a disease of the nation—nay, of humanity—exhibited in individuals. You have gout in your toe, but it is your whole system that is wrong. This disease can be cured by Humanity alone. Criminals are those whom we should pity, should prevent, should isolate, and, if possible, cure.

Remember what John Bradford said, looking on a man going to be hanged: "But for the grace of God there goes John Bradford." He, too, would have been the same had he had bad training in his youth.

We have all of us within us instincts which rightly directed result in good, which in default of outlet we can be trained to control, but which without outlet and without the receipt of training may result in crime. Crime is, therefore, a defect of training and environment, not of personality.

CHAPTER XVI

COURTS REFORM

But, pending any such great change as must come in all penal law when the subject has been carefully studied, there are many smaller amendments that might be made both in Civil and Revenue Courts and Law.

The pressing need in Criminal Procedure is, I think, a change in the treatment of an accused person when he is arrested.

The first instinct of an offender is, as I have said, to confess, even if an understanding person is not available to confess to. He has offended the Law; he wants to make all amends he can by confessing to the representative of that offended Personality. I have seen very many first offenders and talked to them before they got into the hands of pleaders and others, and my experience tells me that a man who has committed his first offence is very like a man who has caught his first attack of serious illness. He is afraid not so much of the results as of the thing itself. Sin has caught him, and he is afraid of sin. He wants protection and help and cure. He does not want to hide anything; his first need is confession to some understanding ear. Many, many such confessions have I heard in the old days. That is the result of the first offence.

But this tendency to truth is choked when it is ascertained that as a result the offender will be vindictively punished and made in the end far worse than he was at the beginning. Naturally the offender says to himself: "I am bad now. What shall I be after two years' gaol? Better fight it out. If I win and get acquitted, at least I shall have a chance to reform. If convicted that chance will be taken from me for ever. And fighting will not lose me anything. The penitent prisoner who confesses gets no lighter punishment than if he had put the Court to the expense of a long trial. Why therefore repent? It will do me harm, not good." That is the case now; under reasonable laws it would be the other way. But even yet in country places he often confesses to the police by whom he is arrested.

Now by Indian Law no confession to the police may be offered in evidence. The reason of this is that the police, in their keenness to secure a conviction, may extort a false confession by torture, and there have been in fact enough of such cases to cause doubt and to prevent the police being allowed to receive a confession. Therefore if the offender wishes to confess he is taken now to a magistrate, there his confession is recorded. Then he is sent back to police custody. He is visited by his relatives, a pleader is engaged for him. His folly in confessing is pointed out to him and he withdraws the confession, alleging that he had been tortured to confess. His confession is not only negatived, but a slur is cast on the police which is hard to remove. Their case and evidence appear tainted, and the accused often secures an acquittal though the Magistrate knows that the confession was true.

All this is very common both in Burma and India, and it is disastrous to allow and to encourage such things, as by our procedure we do encourage them. There should be a complete change.

When a man is arrested some such procedure should be adopted as this:

He should be told by the police that he is being taken direct to the magistrate who will try the case, who will hear anything accused has to say. He should be warned to say nothing to the police. Then he should be taken direct to the magistrate, who should explain to him fully what he is accused of and ask him what he has to say.

Whatever his statement be, the magistrate should tell him that he will himself at once investigate it and summon witnesses; meanwhile the accused should be remitted to custody, but *not* to police custody. That is where all the trouble comes in and all opportunities for making charges against the police. If there be no gaol there should be a lock-up in charge of Indian police who are under the magistrate and are not concerned in the guilt or otherwise of the accused. The investigating police should only have access to accused by permission of the magistrate. He should, however, be allowed to see his friends and a pleader if he wish. But I am sure of this, that the first offender would rather trust the magistrate, if he were a personality who he knew would help him, than any pleader.

Further, if a man confess truly, his punishment should be greatly reduced. I do not say this should be done because he gives less trouble, but because the frame of mind induced by a free and full confession is a sounder frame of mind on which to begin reformation than are defiance and negation, which are now inculcated by our system.

The trial need not wait till the case is complete. The magistrate could summon the police witnesses at once, and he should examine them himself, allowing only the police to suggest questions if they wish. Similarly, with the defence witnesses, they could be examined as they came in and should be examined by the magistrate himself. No one but the magistrate should be allowed to speak directly to any party to the case.

All cross-examination should be absolutely prohibited. If either side have matters they wish brought out of a witness, they should tell the magistrate and he would ask such questions as he thought fit. There is no such curse now to justice as cross-examination by a clever pleader or barrister. It is a sort of forensic show-off by the advocate at the cost of the witness, and frequently at the cost of justice. For, naturally, no one cares to be bullied by a licensed bully, and witnesses consequently will not come to Court if they can help it. When in Court they are bamboozled and made to contradict themselves where they have originally spoken the truth.

I have often been told that acute cross-examination by a clever barrister is the greatest safeguard justice can have from false evidence. I don't believe a word of it.

A magistrate can by far fewer and simpler questions expose false evidence better than an advocate does, because the magistrate is intent only on his business—to find the truth; the advocate is advertising himself, and trying to destroy truth as well as falsehood.

But if the magistrate did all the questioning I don't believe there would be much false evidence. Witnesses will lie to the opposite side, but not to an understanding Court.

Perjury would disappear. What is its present cause? Contempt of the Court and sympathy with either complainant or accused, which sympathy sees no chance of justice for its object except by perjury. Because a trial is a fight. There is not a human being East or West who would not be ashamed to lie to a Court he knew was trying to do its best for all—parties and public. It is because the Courts as at present constituted do as much harm as good that perjury is rampant and condoned. It is so in all countries, it has been so in all periods.

Then, as soon as possible, juries should be introduced. This cannot be done until the law, especially as regards punishment, is greatly altered in accordance with the common sense of the people, but it is the objective to be aimed at as soon as possible. Until the public co-operate with the Courts in all ways you will never have a good system of justice. Crime hurts the people far more than it hurts Government. Don't you think the people know that? And don't you suppose they want it prevented even more than Government does? In any case that is the fact. They hate the Courts now because they don't prevent or cure crime; they only make matters worse.

The only objection I see to this proposed alteration is that it will take more time and so cost more money. At first it may do so, but even then what the public loses by more taxes it will more than save in having to pay less to lawyers. How much unnecessary money is now paid to lawyers? Enough, I am sure, to double the magistracy and then leave a big balance. Courts should be made for the people, not for lawyers. And in time crime would so decrease that there would be saving all round.

The reform of the Civil Courts should follow somewhat the same lines. A man should not have to wait to see a civil judge till his case is all made out. He should be able to go to him at once and confide in him, and the judge should send for the other party and try to make an arrangement between them so that no suit should be filed. Not until that has been done and not unless a judge give a certificate of its necessity should a suit be allowed to be filed as it is now. And then when it is filed the judge should conduct the case and not the advocates on each side. That is the only way to stop the perjury which increases and will increase. Magistrates and judges must cease to be umpires of a combat, and become investigators of truth.

As regards the laws of marriage and inheritance, no great change can be made until there is a real representative Assembly to make these changes, but even there something could be done. That fossilisation of custom described by Sir Henry Sumner Maine should stop. Because a High Court proved a hundred years ago that a certain custom existed there is no evidence that it does or should exist now. To establish precedents of this nature is to stop all progress of every kind; we have a vision different from the poet's

> Of bondage slowly narrowing down
> From precedent to precedent.

Why should not fresh inquiries into custom be made from time to time, it being understood that any Court-ruling only applied to that time and place, and did not bind the future? Something must be done. Things cannot go on as they are. We reproach the Indians for want of progress, but we ourselves are the main cause of that stagnation. We bind them and they cannot move.

As regards land policy there is this to be said, that fixed ideas are a mistake.

In Bengal there was at one time a fixed idea that all land did and must belong to large land-owners, and so, partly out of sheer ignorance, partly out of prejudice, a race of Zemindars was created out of the tax-gatherers to the Mogul Empire. The result has been sad.

Again in Burma the same idea prevailed for a while, and headmen were encouraged to annex communal waste as their private land. This was unfortunate.

Then came a reaction, and all large estates were denounced as bad. There was to be a small tenantry holding direct from Government, forbidden to alienate their land, and all leasing of land to tenants was forbidden.

This I understand to be the policy still. It is a policy of fixed ideas, and as applied to anything that has life, like land tenure, it is unfortunate, no matter what the fixed idea be.

If there be one truth above another that is clear in studying land systems it is that no one permanent system is good. The cultivation of land, like all matters, undergoes evolution and change. What is good to-day may not be good to-morrow. The English system of large estates cultivated by tenants did, at one time in English history, produce the best farming in the world. English farming was held up as an example to all countries and was so admitted by them. The system of large estates allowed of the expenditure of capital, experiments in new cultivations and new breeds of cattle, and variety of crops. It suited its day well. And though its full day has passed, there will never be a time when some large estates will not be able to justify themselves. Even if, as apparently is the case now in England, *petite culture* is that best adapted to the cultivation of the day and the needs of the people, yet there is still room for large estates. A dead uniformity of small holdings could not but be unfortunate for any country.

Further, although excessive alienation of land through money-lenders may be very bad, yet stagnation in ownership may be worse. India and Burma are progressive, and changes must take place. Cultivators will become artisans and traders; city people will like to return to the land. There is an ebb and flow which is good for all. Too great rigidity of system will stop progress. A good system of land tenure is that which is in accordance with the evolution of the people it applies to and assists in that evolution.

While recognising that for the bulk of the people small holdings are best, it will not forbid larger estates; while admitting that the alienation of land through borrowing recklessly from money-lenders is bad, it will see that the progress of the people from purely agricultural towards a state of industrial activity is not checked. It takes all sorts to make a State.

It may be good for the cultivator to hold direct from Government, but if Government is to be the landlord it must act up to its name. It must give compensation for improvements when a tenant has to relinquish the land. Otherwise no tenant will improve, and the necessity for improvement, for wells, irrigation, embankments, manuring, and so on, is the greatest necessity of agriculture. In my own experience I have seen that the system of State land tenure in Upper Burma does stop improvements.

That is the light in which the land question has to be worked out, on broad comprehensive lines—that, while acknowledging the present, sees also the future, which, while seeing one form of good does not deny another.

So, with an understanding and a sympathetic *personnel*, the administration would be brought nearer to the people, until at length when their capacity for self-government had developed they would be able to take over our administrative machine little by little and work it themselves.

They could never do that now. If by any chance they did get possession of the machinery at present, they would set to work to smash it till none remained.

CHAPTER XVII

SELF-GOVERNMENT

And thus the sheltering Government of India having been reformed both in its *personnel* and in its laws, brought into touch and sympathy with its people, a start would be made with self-government.

That, of course, must begin with the village, which is the germ from which all self-government that is of any value has always begun, and on the health and vitality of which it must always depend. The village organism must be restored to the state in which we found it, and from that be helped and encouraged to grow to greater things.

The whole of the present conception of the village as an appanage of the headman, and the conception of the headman as an official of Government, must be swept away and a new and true conception must be arrived at.

The village is a self-contained organism, and the headman is its representative before Government and its executive head, the real power being in the Council. Powers and responsibility reside in the village as a whole and in no individual. The people must not be ruled, but rule themselves.

Now as to the exact way in which this conception should be carried out it is impossible to say. In each Province—in distinct parts of the same Province—the village system assumed different forms to meet different circumstances. In Madras the village community was in many details different from that in Burma, and in the North-West still more so. Therefore, the particular way in which the conception should be realised would vary greatly. And only by experience could a satisfactory form for each Province be evolved. Neither would it be possible even in Burma to go back to the old form exactly. Events have marched since then, and what was satisfactory thirty or more years ago would not be so now. The villages must not be reconstituted by copying the past; they must be constituted anew, maintaining, however, the spirit of the past and giving scope for evolution in the future.

Therefore, the scheme that I am about to unfold must be taken to be merely tentative and apply only to Burma. The principles are, I think, right; the details must, of course, be discovered by experience. Practice alone would show how far they realised the objective that is to be aimed at—the constitution of a village organism on natural lines that would govern itself without any need for interference and would be able to grow and evolve.

My scheme is as follows:

In every village a Council should be constituted and the headman should be its executive head.

How this Council should be constituted I do not know. I think there should be wards, each of which should have an elder, representative of the people, but no rigid system of election should be laid down. I have found that villages and wards can very often appoint a representative man by general consent, which is much better than by election. That should only occur in case of a dead-lock. The Council should itself define the wards, and it should be allowed to co-opt additional members. All representation by class or religion should be prohibited. The unit is not so many people, but a section of a village—neighbours dwelling together and whose interests are thereby united. Appointment to the Council should be indefinite; that is to say, an elder should remain an elder until he resigned or until the ward turned him out. I don't think they would like continual elections. An election is a bad means to a desired end—that of obtaining the best representative. And in small communities the sense is usually apparent without it.

The headman should be chosen by the Council from among its members and his election confirmed by Government. His appointment should be according to the wish of the Council, that is to say, for life, unless he resigned or the Council turned him out. He should be responsible to the Council. The Council, as representing the village, should be responsible to Government, and it would always be possible for the Deputy Commissioner to bring pressure on a recalcitrant Council by threatening to suspend the constitution and place the village under an appointed headman for a time if they did not carry out their duties properly.

To this village community should be handed over certain duties, rights, and responsibilities, much what the headman has now, the collection of revenue, etc. All civil, criminal, and revenue cases under certain values and of certain denominations should be handed over to them to try; that is to say, that cognisance should be refused by our police and our Courts, so that the parties could go to the Village Council if they liked. There should be no appeal from the decisions of the Council, no advocates should be allowed, and no record should be required. All penalties imposed should be paid into the village fund.

This fund should exist for all villages, and its nucleus should be, say, half an anna in the rupee of the revenue collections, to which should be added fines, special rates which the Council should be empowered to impose for specific purposes, and other forms of revenue which would vary from place to place. I think a percentage of the district fund should be given to them. A rate on inhabited houses—a rent on house sites—would be a good way of raising money. The purposes for which the fund could be used would be water-supply, sanitation, roads, lighting, watchmen, and so on. Simple account-books would have to be kept, and these accounts would have to be audited once a year.

Model schemes for sanitation, village roads, etc., could be made out for each village to live up to as fast as it could.

Further, villages should have the power to carry out irrigation works on their own initiative and under their own control. I consider this a most important proviso, because I know many villages where this could be done by the village, whereas it is not possible to individuals. I also know one recent case in my district where it was done with great success by the headman and elders. I got them a small grant, and I often went to see how the work was getting on, but I never interfered in any way, and the result was most satisfactory. There was at first a difficulty about collecting the rates, because there was no legal system under which a man who used the water could be made to pay. However, this also settled itself.

Irrigation works, roads, and bridges are most necessary to many villages, but now, unless Government carry out the work, there is no one to do it. And Government will not carry out small works.

It is by the execution of such works that the village would prosper and the village fund grow. Loans should be granted for these purposes by Government, to be repaid out of the profits.

Before our annexation all works were executed by the villages, and the considerable irrigation works in many places are evidence of their ability. All this initiative has now been killed. Yet it is a most valuable asset, not only materially, but morally.

As regards this fund, it will, I know, be objected by many people that it will be simply an excuse for peculation. "Orientals," they say, "cannot be honest, and the funds would be misappropriated right and left."

Exactly this same charge was made when the Co-operative Credit Banks were started. Their history will sufficiently refute such an absurdity. Orientals are just as honest as any other people, and, given a good system, village funds will no more be stolen in India or Burma than municipal funds are in England.

In organising these villages there is another point to be borne in mind. In that desperate struggle after rigid uniformity which distinguishes the Indian Government, every separate hamlet in Burma was put under a separate headman, and thus made a separate organism.

Now it may be that occasionally the village was too large, and a division was needed, but in many other cases the disintegration of long-established units was severely felt. Several hamlets may have one interest in common. They may be grouped round a small irrigation work, or along a stream, or have a fishery in common, or be in other matters of great use to each other. If run as separate organisms there is bound to be strife, each trying for his own benefit. If allowed to remain one organism they will be not only more peaceful, but stronger, and better able to manage their affairs. Thus the rigid formulæ of Government in this matter as in others should give place to common sense.

Further: in future, villages should be allowed to coalesce if mutual interests attract them. Two or three villages if allowed to combine would carry out works that one could not do.

I see no great difficulty in Burma in thus restoring the organism of village life. It would require mainly tact on the part of the District Officer and ability to let alone. His tendency now is always to interfere if he can. His rule should be never to interfere if he can help it. When things go wrong persistently it will probably be found that there is something amiss with the way the village is organised, and that it requires some slight modification. If a horse can't draw a cart it is better to see what is wrong with the horse or the cart than try to move them both along by turning the wheels round yourself. You won't get far that way. The more you push the more the horse will jib. And Village Councils will be very willing horses if let alone and the cart be not too cumbersome or the hill they have to climb too steep. But they must be left alone. Read the history of municipal institutions in England and note the principles. They are universal.

Once the village communities are strong and healthy, a further step could be made by instituting a township or sub-divisional Council, and later a District Council.

For these I am not prepared to offer any suggestions. It would require a very careful study of local conditions and of the people, a wide experience gained from the working of the resuscitated villages, to know how these should be constituted and what powers and responsibilities should be entrusted to them. I think a sound analogy might be obtained from a study of English counties—not so much perhaps as they are now, but as they were—in spirit, not in law.

After the village organism was established, perhaps in order to its proper establishment, a local Government Board would have to be created. This would have to be in time entirely native to the Province. It is, I think, essential that it should be so. What its relations with the District Officer would be I do not know. I foresee difficulties. It is essential for good order in the district that there be no one between the head and the people. Nevertheless, I don't think he could establish and work the village organism himself. I think he would be too tempted to interfere; and, moreover, there would have to be a certain co-ordination between the systems in various districts. They need not be the same in detail, but the idea should be the same. That is because eventually they must coalesce into bigger organisms. But a District Officer with a strong personality would, I think, be liable to impress that personality on the village, and as it must be self-governing that might create difficulties. For as the villages increased the District Officer would decrease. Gradually his powers would devolve on the local organisms. There would thus be a certain rivalry between the District Officer and the local organisms, which, if the officer were the head of both, might result in injury to the latter. Perhaps some such relation as exists between the Land Records Department and the District Officer would be possible. The Land Records has its own organisation, which works independently of the district but in harmony with it. All this, however, is not a matter which can be thought out. It will have to be worked out, and a correct system can only come little by little, experience showing how modifications should be made. I do not see any great difficulty provided there are common sense and unity of aim on both sides.

And from districts—when they had settled down into distinct organisms more or less self-governing—representatives, not delegates, could be sent to a Provincial Council. Then you would have a real Council, one representative of the people because proceeding from the people, not less surely because not directly. I am not sure that direct election such as is practised in England and America, for instance, does cause representation of the people. In England, at all events, it is not so now. The only power the people have now is to choose between the delegates of two or more parties. Beyond this they have no voice nor choice. They cannot find any expression for their own wishes. Their member may be, probably is, a man they never heard of before the "Party" sent him to contest the seat. There is, in fact, in England to-day no real representation of the people at all. By people, of course, I mean the people as a whole, including all classes. But under some such scheme as I have sketched out for Burma there would be real representation of the people, of localities as a whole, units; local men acquainted with the local conditions would be chosen and not pleaders, and the locality would hold them responsible. Thus the opinion of such a Council would represent the wishes of the people; it could be depended on, and to it could considerable powers be delegated permanently. It would, in fact, in time constitute a Provincial Government in federal relations with the other Provincial Governments. That is the only possible way that a real government can be built up.

And it must always be remembered that the basis is the Village. On the health of the Village all other things depend; from the healthy working of the Village all things may proceed. It is the first but not last word in local self-government.

A very integral part of any self-government is Education, and to that I come in the next chapter.

CHAPTER XVIII

EDUCATION

To the success of any form of self-government a good education is absolutely essential; that a people should be able to exercise self-government it is necessary that they be educated to self-government; for this capacity no more comes by itself than ability to build a ship or steer it when built. And as the government must be self-government, so the education must be a national education and not an imported one.

I have already had something to say on this subject in former chapters when writing of the Indian civilian, and the principles which underlie good education are the same everywhere. A well-educated man is he in whom his mental and physical powers have been so brought out that he can face the ordinary vicissitudes of his life with confidence, that he can understand them and combat them materially to the best of his ability, and that when materially defeated he may still rise spiritually above all defeat and discouragement. Education is necessary to everyone—man or woman, peasant or prince, merchant or artisan—and that man is best educated who can make the best of his life whatever its station may be.

Thus it will be seen that education is mainly relative. A man who would be well educated if in one station of life would be hopelessly ignorant if in another. I doubt if Whewell would have been considered educated had fate suddenly made him a soldier, a political officer on a frontier, or a cultivator. A keen eye gained by experience for market fluctuations is better for a merchant than all the learning of all the libraries.

But this specialisation belongs properly to higher education. There are certain foundation principles necessary to any success in life, to being able to live it in whatever station with dignity and with prosperity. What are those principles?

I think the Indian Education Department would say that these are reading, writing, and arithmetic—that is to say, acquirements. I should say they are qualities of character.

What are these qualities?

First and foremost is belief in his own people, not his caste or his creed, but in the people who inhabit his Province, who will eventually make up his nationality. If the man is to do good work for his people the boy must desire to do good work—he must have a certainty in the unlimited possibilities of his people, that though they may be young now they will grow to a world stature. Therefore, that it is his duty to help them. He must be sure that this world is good—to be made better by him and his fellows and his descendants. He has inherited much; he must hand on more. He has no right to live unless he does his duty to life and in life—that is to say, he must have a purpose in life, for without a purpose life cannot be lived.

Secondly, he must see that to the accomplishment of his purpose, which is but part of the World's Purpose, he must cultivate two qualities, obedience in act and freedom of thought. He must learn to obey, because he must see for himself that only by men acting together under authority can anything be achieved. His obedience will then be a willing and cheerful obedience, because necessary to his own purpose. He must obey that later he may be obeyed. He must keep his mind free, because to admit authority in thought is to kill thought. He must see things for himself and judge for himself, that when he is able to act for himself he may do so on truth and not on hearsay. He must learn to respect the opinions of others which they have founded also on experience, while not necessarily adopting them, because he may see things differently.

He must learn self-knowledge to recognise what he can do and what he can't.

He should cultivate self-command that must not mean self-extinction.

On a base like this all other things come naturally.

Is there any such ideal in elementary education in India? I can safely say that there is no such ideal. All that the Department seeks to do is to stuff a child with reading, writing, and arithmetic, and other learning, regardless of his character or his objective in life.

Therefore elementary education is not popular in Burma, because it seems to have no good purpose.

That was true of education before we took the country. It was then mainly, for boys, in the hands of monks, and I do not think that education when controlled by religion has been popular anywhere in the world. It has been accepted because there was no other means of education available, but it was not admired. Our Government has accepted the monastery schools, and it has also encouraged lay schools, but neither seem to give much satisfaction.

Now this is not the place to discuss religion of any kind, and I have no intention of entering into such a vexed question. There are good things in all religions—borrowed from humanity; there are doubtful things; there are bad things. But the foundation of every religion is a declaration that this world is evil and that we should despise it. Now the objective of all education is to fit a boy for his life, and he cannot be so fit if he despise life. He must love it, admire it, desire in all ways to help it, to increase it, beautify it. His objective must be in this life. Further, the tendency of all faiths is to raise barriers between races and castes. But it is an essential part of any true education that a boy understand that in striving for the good of the community he must ignore all differences. Humanity is one, and the God of Humanity is One, whatever faiths may say.

Thus religions when mixed with education have a paralysing effect. I have often heard this said in Burma. Here is a conversation I once had at a village I knew very well. It occurred, as did most of the talks I had with the people, just after sunset, when I had my chair set outside my rest-house, and the people came dropping in to gossip. There were a number of people, the headman, elders, their wives and children, and two monks from a neighbouring monastery. They talked quite freely because they knew that after office hours I forgot I was an official, or even an Englishman, and just talked to them as one human being to another. I may add that I had been inspecting the village school where little boys and girls learned together. I had also been to a monastery where the elder boys went.

"Well," I said, "what is the news?"

There was an expectant silence. Evidently there was some news; the question was—who should tell it?

"What is it, Headman?" I asked.

The Headman rubbed an ankle reflectively. "The fact is," he answered, "there is no news that would interest your Honour; only just village doings, foolish doings."

"Hum," I said; "that sounds to me as if a young man had been doing something."

Several of the men smiled—"Possibly with the assistance of a girl"—and I glanced at some girls. They giggled, and the Headman said briefly:

"Maung Ka's son has run off with a girl."

"Oh!" I said, turning to Maung Ka, whom I knew well enough—a tall, fine-looking man, who was looking very gloomy. "It's a way boys have. There's no harm in it."

"Not if he can support her afterwards," said Maung Ka gruffly.

"Can't he do that?" I asked.

It appeared he couldn't. He had spent all his boyhood in a monastery "learning" till his father fetched him out. Then he went to the other extreme and levanted with a girl. "He doesn't know one end of a bullock from the other," said the father; "he can't plough or sow; he can't work; he has no common sense. That's what schooling does for a boy."

Most of the other men agreed with him, and we had a discussion on education, in which everyone took part.

The general opinion was that schooling should be to fit you for life. The monks said for eternity, but the villagers—though out of respect for the monks they said little—evidently didn't make any such distinction. What wasn't fit for time wasn't fit for eternity. Reading, writing, and arithmetic were good, because a boy needed these. Beyond that they seemed to think schooling did harm. A boy learned more from his father and the other villagers than from school. As to a girl, "What," asked an elder indignantly, "is the use of a girl learning to write? What will she write? Love-letters only."

"Well," I asked, "and isn't that good—for the boy who gets them?"

The fact is, the villagers are plain, common-sense men and women, and what they want for their children is that they be better fitted for the struggle of life. They do not observe that to be the case at present. They judge by results, and the results are not good, they say.

In fact, except as to the actual acquisition of reading, writing, and arithmetic, which may or may not be of much use, the teaching—and still more than the teaching, the influence—is bad. It unfits for life, it gives wrong ideals, or it kills all ideals.

The higher education is, I think, worse. It follows an imported system, and in the importation all the good is left out. In England a boy's real education comes from association with the other boys and from his father. From them he learns whatever he does learn of conduct, of ambition to true ends, of acting in concert, of ability to judge for himself and stick up for himself.

In India a wrong ideal has been conceived from the beginning. It has been assumed, tacitly maybe, that an Englishman is the final and completely perfected work of God and man, and that all nations should copy him and try to become, if not a sterling Englishman, at least an electro-plate one.

That is disastrous. It depresses the people by depreciating their own races and holding up an objective which is impossible, and if possible would be wrong.

There are in the pasts of nearly all Oriental people ideals which are quite as good as ours, and far better fitted for them. Are these ever taught to them? India once led the civilisation of the world; is that past ever brought up and explained and realised for them? Never, I think.

Further, higher education to be of any use must be objective. You must know what you want the boy to be. What does Government want the products of its higher education to be? I have no idea. Has the Government?

Of what use are these products of the higher education in India? They are useful but for two things, to be lawyers or pleaders, or to be clerks. They are dealers in words, and not in facts or in humanity.

Government accepts a certain number into its service, because the first ideal of Government is a man who can fill up forms and returns, speedily, accurately, and punctually. They can do that. When they have district work to do they fail, because they have no personality, no freedom of thought, and because the people despise them. The old officials whom we took over from the Burmese Government, whatever their defects, had "auza"—personality. It is a commonplace to say that the Burmese have deteriorated. That is not true. They have as much potentiality as before, but this potentiality is wiped out by "education." Far from being really educated, they are merely stuffed, and their natural abilities stifled. Moreover, they cease to be Burmans, or Madrassis, or Bengalis, and become a sort of hybrid. This is due to their English masters, who are obsessed with the idea that the only way to "educate" anyone is to turn him into a plaster Englishman. I have had some experience of these unfortunate boys who have taken degrees.

Personally, if I had to administer a difficult district, I should choose my Burmese assistants from men who had never been to school, and to satisfy Government I would engage some B.A.'s and F.A.'s to be their clerks and fill up the forms. I should be sorry for the B.A.'s, because I think they have as good stuff in them as the others, but their want of education has unfitted them for work requiring "auza."

That is really what it amounts to; the school-trained boy is not educated, whereas the boy brought up in contact with the world is perforce educated. The first is a hothouse plant; the second a useful field plant.

I am aware that current opinion puts down the failure of the educated young Indian to his want of religion. He has been educated out of his own faith and not accepted into any other; hence his want of character. Of all the wild shibboleths about India and the Indians this is, I think, the wildest. That a man is injured by being brought to see the foolishness of caste, of infant marriage, of harems and zenanas, of all the forms and ceremonies with which all religions are covered, seems to me a triumph of illogic. Only the "Occidental mind" at its best could conceive such an idea. In so far as education destroys these ideas it does good. Wherein it harms him is by taking him apart from his people, rendering him not desirous to help them but to disown them. He is taught that to be an Englishman should be his ideal—that he "should cultivate English habits of thought"—as if true thought had any habits—so that, finally, he can't think at all. He is directed to wrong ideals; he is rendered unhappy; he is *dépaysé*; he is useless for any work, except being a clerk or lawyer; he has no more character than a jelly-fish. Instead of wishing to lead his people he wishes to identify himself with the English Government, be a civilian, and rule his people. He should be filled with a boundless confidence in the future of his people, and that it is his duty to help that future to be realised. He is discouraged and rendered hopeless. Instead of being a help he is the greatest danger his own people will have to meet when they move forward. He is a danger to all.

The Education Department of the Government of India is the new Frankenstein, and the Higher Education is its monster. The students have sunk under their "education," and in consequence they are unhappy. Who wonders? But, in fact, an alien Power cannot introduce or work any real system of education. It must be indigenous—something of the soil, and not exotic. It, like self-government, must begin with small things in the village and gradually rise.

Like all things, if it is to live and prosper and extend it must have a soul. And the soul of education, like the soul of life, is an emotion tending towards a *desired* end. The desired end of education is the rise and progress not merely of the individual but of the nation. That has been the soul of the progress of Japan; that must be the soul of the progress of any people; and education will only be enthusiastically taken up when it is seen to be a means to that end.

Such an education cannot be given by Englishmen. Any Education Department must be Provincial and draw its vigour from below. It must not be a machine governed from Simla with text-books as thumbscrews and manuals as beds of

Procrustes.

Before there can be a real Education Department it must be entirely native of the Province, responsible to the Province for its success. Can we create such a Department? I think we could, slowly, by handing our village schools as much as possible to Village Councils, district schools to District Councils, and the University to the head Provincial Assembly when it comes into being. They will each have to think out what result they want, and then how to attain that result.

But all must begin with the village; within it alone is the germ cell of all future progress.

CHAPTER XIX

CONCLUSION

There are many other subjects connected with the renaissance of India that I should like to enter into, but I cannot do so here. This book is already too full of matter that is never easy, and is sometimes controversial. Such subjects are the real ideals and ideas that underlay the religions of India, Hindu, and Mohammedan, and which gave them life until they were hidden under priest-made ritual and killed; the early history of India as a history of ideas and civilisations, and not a stupid agglomeration of battles and intrigues; the absolute necessity, as shown in all history, of representation and legislation being by territory, and not by class, nor race, nor religion; and there are many others. Perhaps some day I may return to these matters, or, more happily, other writers will undertake them. They will see the interest and pleasure to be derived from the study of humanity and ideas, and will leave on one side the dusty frippery of ceremonies and creeds and customs, of the details of battles and palace intrigues and dynasties. Life lies under all these things, and they but affect it as old clothes do a man. Meanwhile, I have done what I can to show the causes of the trouble in India and to indicate in what way it may be met.

Only in some such way as that I have sketched, only by following principles of the nature here indicated, can the Government of India be drawn into accordance with the people. The Government must learn to understand those many millions over whom it has acquired so great a power, and in understanding them acquire sympathy with their desires and needs. The people must learn to know, and recognise, and feel that Government does understand them; that it has sympathy with them, and will help them onward to that goal whither their Destiny is calling them. So will both work together toward that end.

To conquer India was great; it is the one great deed whereby we shall live in history; but to make of India a daughter, not a subject, to help her grow out of our care till she is strong enough to walk alone, that will be greater still.

No nation in the world's history has ever done a deed like that.

To conquer India required great courage, it required ability of the highest, it needed self-denial, self-sacrifice of the individual for the nation. What will the freedom of India need in us? It will need qualities higher even than these are. It will need courage, as great as or greater even than that which we have shown before—the courage to leave alone; it will require self-abnegation and self-sacrifice, not for our own nation, but for India, for Humanity; it will require a sympathy and understanding such as no nation has ever yet felt for a foreign people.

Can we do this?

I do not know. Can we with whom representation except of the wire-pullers of the party has ceased to exist, in whose schools of all kinds and in whose universities there is no education, whose legal system is bad beyond all expression, who have under free forms less real freedom than most other countries, can we give to India what we have not? I think that we shall have to take the beam out of our own eye first. Are we prepared to do that?

What will it need in India? It will need courage too, it will need self-restraint not less than that which we shall have to show, the courage to go slowly, to restrain the rising tide within the banks of safety, to so direct it that the flood will fertilise, not destroy.

It will need more than this. What ruined India twice, and what ruins her now? Division. Race, caste and creed are curses when they make one man despise or hate another. There is one God. Brahma and Allah and Jehovah are but names for One if truly seen. His kingdom is in neither Church nor creed nor Prophet, neither in temple nor in holy place, but in the hearts of men—all men. If you read truly you will see that in the beginning all religions were ideas, great streams of hope and truth driving to one ideal. All truth which is a living truth is One. But formulæ and castes and creeds and ceremonies and forms, rites of all kinds, are priest-made things that kill and petrify. All souls come here from God; not Brahmin souls nor Pongyis' souls nor Christian souls alone, but every soul in every man that lives, they come from God and so return. They are part with us of the eternal "I" in which are lost all "yous" or "theys." Can the Brahmins forget their legendary pride and prove their vaunted worth by leading India to an equal freedom and not keeping her back by the slavery they have thrown upon her? Can the Moslem, casting off the mould of dead tradition, remember the Omniades, their tolerance, their wisdom, their civilisation; what they did and, above all, what they did not do?

Can the Buddhist believe that life is good—not evil; to be made the most of, not feared nor shunned? to be loved and lived?

I do not know. These things are all upon the knees of God.

But for a real new India to arise all these things must come to pass. She is now India Irredenta. And to be redeemed all Indians must offer up as sacrifice, not their good things, but all those evil things they cling to blindly—their hates and their divisions, their pride in what they should be thoroughly ashamed of, their quarrels and misunderstandings. There were a sacrifice that God would love.

Will it come to pass? Who knows? We can only do our best—all of us.

Printed by Libri Plureos GmbH in Hamburg,
Germany